Junior Class of Washington College

The Alpha

Junior Class of Washington College

The Alpha

ISBN/EAN: 9783337089450

Printed in Europe, USA, Canada, Australia, Japan

Cover: Foto ©ninafisch / pixelio.de

More available books at **www.hansebooks.com**

THE
ALPHA,

PUBLISHED BY THE

JUNIOR CLASS,

OF

WASHINGTON COLLEGE,

1895.

CHESTERTOWN TRANSCRIPT.
STEAM JOB PRINT, 1895.

To the memory of
REV. WILLIAM SMITH, A. M., D. D.,
The first President of Washington College, the profound
scholar and illustrious divine, to whose far-seeing
statesmanship the establishment of Washington College, and the organization of
higher education in the Middle
States, are due more than
to the exertion of
any other single
individual.
The editors respectfully dedicate this volume.

Editorial Staff.

Editor-in-Chief,
EDWARD M. NOBLE.

Assistant Editors,
M. BELLE BOSTON, MARY BURCHINAL,
M. EARLE USILTON, H. ARRINGDALE JUMP.

Alumni Editor,
R. LEE GLOVER.

Business Manager,
CHARLES W. EASLEY.

Assistant Manager.
E. RIGBY McDORMAN.

Poet.
SAMUEL R. DOUGLAS.

Introductory.

IT IS with some natural misgiving, that we present to the public this, the first attempt of Washington College to compete with sister institutions in the line of undergraduate literature. This feeling is strengthened rather than lessened, from a consciousness of the fact that the audience to whom we address ourselves, while limited in number, is in a position to pass critical judgment upon the merits and demerits of our work, as to whether it truly represents, or otherwise, the esprit of the college from which it emanates. Yet, this circumstance is not without its recompense; for we feel that whatever our weaknesses may be, they will be freely pardoned by those who, before us, have made to echo the corridors of old Washington.

In these pages an attempt is made to present a view of our ALMA MATER as she is to-day, though glimpses are taken at our historic and interesting past. These backward glances reveal in a clearer light our present position, and from a comparison of the two we may learn if we are keeping abreast, in our particular sphere with the foremost in the grand progressive march of American schools. Our record is without blemish; we believe our future will be equally beyond reproach, and from a material standpoint, far more brilliant and influential. Between the vanished months with their fading memories and years that are yet to be, we stand to-day, glorying in the first, enthusiastic for the second.

And as we gaze about us, we have attempted to put in enduring form the sights which meet our view, leavening the whole with a cursory backward glance and a peep into the possible future.

We believe no one will question the need, or the practical utility of this volume. There exists a niche, long vacant, which it endeavors to fill. How snugly, we must leave to others to judge. Aside from other considerations which may have influenced us, we have felt within ourselves the want of a publication of this kind, to aid in crystallizing the progressive spirit now existent among our students, and in consummating it into permanent and continuous advancement.

When the idea of publishing an annual was first broached we thought the suggestion good. Yet, not until the matter assumed more practical shape, did we feel the full weight of the responsibility resting upon us. As our work has progressed, we have realized even more fully that, as pioneers in the movement, the result of our labor would be dissected and discussed from many and various points of view.

A brief reference to the reasons actuating us to throw ourselves into the breach, and cause the issue of this publication, may not be without interest. Our excuse, if excuse it may be called, is threefold.

Primarily, we wished to bring in closer contact the alumni and present students. Nothing could be more desirable and more advantageous than to instill into our students a respect and veneration for those men who, in years now past, have hastened forth at the ringing of the chapel bell; or, on the other hand, inculcate in the minds of our graduates a living interest in the present status of the college and the life of its students. Memory is often a treacherous bond, and it behooves us to strengthen it by any available method. It may be that in the absence of any tie of a material kind, many of our graduates have lost to some extent a desirable, and, possibly, an earnest and aggressive interest in the welfare of the college. We know of nothing better calculated to renew and brighten that interest than a volume such as this.

In the next instance, our sister institutions in the State have set us a pace, and we must either keep to it, or lag hopelessly behind. The latter we cannot consent to do. It is not that the issuance of an annual manifests any special enterprise, but that the non-performance of this act on the part of a college displays retrogression or stagnation. To neither of these two very undesirable qualities do we care to confess.

Finally, and candidly, we wish to show the world what we can accomplish; what we are doing here at Washington College. This may be selfish, but if so, it is wholly pardonable, and to the equitable minded, a healthy and desirable ambition.

With this, we present to you the initial product of our brains and hands. It has its faults, perhaps many. Judge them kindly, and accept our earnest assurance that none exist which the best intentions and hard work could eliminate

Washington College.

ORGANIZED BY THE LEGISLATURE OF MARYLAND,

1782.

PRESIDENTS.

1782, Rev. William Smith, D. D.
1816, Rev. Joseph G. Cooper, A. M.
1817, Gerald E. Stack.
1817, Rev. Francis Waters, A. M., D. D.
1823, Rev. Timothy Clowes, A. M., LL. D
1829, Peter Clarke, A. M.
1832, Richard W. Ringgold, A. M.
1854, Rev. Francis Waters, A. M., D. D.
1860, Rev. Andrew J. Sutton, A. M.
1867, R. C. Berkely.
1873, William J. Rivers, A. M.
1887, Thomas N. Williams, A. M.
1889, Charles W. Reid, A. M., Ph. D.

College Calendar.

FALL TERM, '94.

SEPTEMBER 19-20—Examinations for Admission.
    "   19—Fall term begins.
    "   22—Reorganization of Societies.
NOVEMBER 29-30—Thanksgiving Vacation.
DEC. 24—JAN'Y 4—Christmas Vacation.
JANUARY   25—Senior Orations.
    "   26—Annual Banquet of Philomathean Society.
JAN. 28—FEB. 6—Examinations.

SPRING TERM, '95.

FEBRUARY   6—Spring term begins.
    "   22—Celebration of Washington's Birthday.
    "   22—Annual Banquet of Mt. Vernon Society
APRIL   10-17—Easter Vacation.
MAY   17—Senior Orations.
    "   20—Senior's Final Examination.
JUNE   5—Examination of other classes.
    "   16—Baccalaureate Sermon.
    "   16—Annual Sermon of College Y. M. C. A
    "   17—Reception of Piera Society.
    "   17—Anniversary of Mt. Vernon Society
    "   18—Declamation Contest.
            18—Annual Field Day.
            18—Anniversary of Philomathean Society
            18—Alumni Banquet.
            19—Commencement Exercises.
            19—Commencement Ball.

WASHINGTON COLLEGE.

Sketch of Washington College.

In 1780 the charter of the College of Philadelphia, of which Rev. William Smith, D. D., was president, was revoked. The reverend gentleman was induced to take charge of the parish of Chestertown, for the consideration of 600 bushels of wheat per annum. He made such a favorable impression upon the people, that he was speedily elected principal of the Kent county school. He was a born educator, and soon enrolled 140 students. Through his influence, action was taken by the Visitors to obtain from the Legislature a college charter for the Kent county school. That body at their next session, enacted that it would be granted, if $14,000 should be raised in five years, and that the institution should be named Washington College, in grateful remembrance of the illustrious commander-in-chief of the armies of the United States. Within five months the money was all contributed, and the charter was accordingly bestowed. The State, in addition, agreed thereafter forever to pay annually to Washington College £1250 in currency, or $3333. This was to be paid either in Spanish dollars or merchantable wheat or tobacco.

The Western Shore could not endure that the Eastern Shore should have superior educational advantages. Accordingly, in 1784, St. John's College was chartered. At the same time it was enacted, that the two institutions should constitute the University of Maryland, the Governor of the State being chancellor, and one of the principals vice-chancellor. Three attempts were made, about 1790, to bring about a convocation, which was to meet annually, alternately at each college, for the purpose of making common by-laws and bringing the two institutions into close sympathy. Each attempt was a failure, on account of the jealousy existing between the two Shores, and the plan was finally abandoned.

In 1783, the first commencement in Maryland was held at Washington College. There were six graduates, who aired their learning in a Latin and a French oration and a Latin disputation. On the next day, the corner-stone of the college building was laid by Governor Paca with appropriate ceremonies. It was 160 feet long and three stories high. The central portion was 40 feet wide and 100 feet deep, with a hall through the centre from north to south. Each wing was 60 feet by 60 feet, with central halls running north and south. $28,000 were raised for the construction of this building, all of which was contributed by the people of the Eastern Shore, except $200 raised in the three eastern counties of Virginia, and 50 guineas given by General Washington. It afforded ample accommodations for 500 students; yet, it was not completed at'the opening of the nineteenth century. It is doubtful whether it was finished very long before its destruction by fire.

General Washington was present at the second commencement in 1784. The students played before him the tragedy of Gustavus Vasa. At the close of the performance, Dr. Smith said: "You have just performed a play illustrative of the life and actions of Gustavus Vasa; behold here the Gustavus of America!" In 1787, the college conferred upon the Father of His Country the honorary title of L.L. D.

The total expenses in the new institution, were for board, $60; for tuition, $16; room-rent, $5; $81 per annum in all. The standard of scholarship was high. It embraced algebra, geometry, trigonometry, conic sections, fluxious, navigation, surveying, natural philosophy, chemistry, astronomy, moral philosphy, logic, metaphysics, rhetoric, and extensive reading of Greek and Latin authors.

Dr. Smith returned in due time to the college of Philadelphia, and the young institution began to lose ground. In 1796 the building, being still unfinished, was in a deplorable state of decay, and the number of students had fallen to 40.

About 1800 the idea had become rooted in Maryland, that the public money should be devoted to secondary, and not to advanced education. Against this sentiment, Washington College, notwithstanding the contract with the State, waged for a long time an unequal war. Although its doors were never closed, yet it degenerated into an academy. In 1832, it had but a single teacher. Its history and prosperity are indissolubly connected with the State appropriation, as it had no other source of revenue, except the scanty sums received from tuition. From 1805 to 1812, the appropriation was entirely withdrawn. From 1812—1834, it received $800 per annum. From 1834--48, it received $500 per year, $300 having been taken for an academy at Millington. From 1848--56, $2,000 per annum were given. The principle now commenced to gain ground in the State, that the real welfare of the republic depended upon advanced, as well as secondary education. From 1856--70, $3000 were given; from 1870--74, $3,375 was appropriated. From 1874 to 1891, the college received $5,375 per annum, but was compelled to educate 15 students from the Eastern Shore counties, free of all expense. In 1891 the number of free students was increased to 18, or two from each county, with a corresponding increase in the appropriation.

Other attempts were made to improve the financial condition of the college. In 1825, a lottery scheme was instituted and sanctioned by the Legislature, through which $80,000 were to be raised. From this the college realized $20,000.

Unfortunately, in 1827, the college building was destroyed by fire. The college was then removed to the town, and occupied two different houses in succession, neither of which is now standing. In 1844, the present central building was completed, and the college again took possession of "Mount Washington." In 1854, the east and the west hall were completed. These buildings were erected during the presidency of Richard W. Ringgold.

Discipline was in old times, administered with a firm hand in Washington College. Prior to 1823, the crooked morals of refractory students, under 15 years of age, were straightened with a ruler; but at that time a law was passed by the Visitors, by which the ferule could be laid on all students regardless of age or class. At one time, absence from roll-call was punished by a fine not to exceed $5, and other offenses were punished with appropriate levies on the students' purse. When the college commenced to board the students in 1819, trouble arose. This culminated in 1821 in the "grub riot." The board of Governors and Visitors being petitioned, decreed that the students should have fresh meat at least three times a week. When there was no fresh meat, there was to be a light dessert. It was further enacted, that the boys should have as many cups of coffee as they wanted. Thus peace was restored.

In 1889, a preparatory course extending over two years, was put into successful operation. In that year, 70 students were enrolled. In 1890, two residences (one for the principal, the other for the vice-principal, were erected. All the buildings were put in excellent order. The east hall was now made a dormitory for students. In 1891, women were admitted as students of the college, on the same terms as men. In 1892, a handsome gymnasium was erected by the alumni and friends of the college in Chestertown, at a cost of $4200. The Board of Governors and Visitors furnished it with suitable apparatus, at an outlay of about $500. Each class is required to have three exercises a week in the gymnasium, under the instruction of the director. Since 1893, a lady has occupied the chair of Modern Languages. Since 1889, the average yearly enrollment has been considerably over one hundred.

Board of Trustees.

Hon. JOSEPH A. WICKES, President.

JAMES A. PEARCE, A. M., Secretary.

COLIN F. STAM, A. M.,	Chestertown, Md.
RICHARD W. JONES, A. M.,	Rock Hall, Md.
SAMUEL BECK, M. D.,	Chestertown, Md.
WM. N. E. WICKES,	Chestertown, Md.
WILLIAM S. WALKER,	Chestertown, Md.
N. W. COMEGYS,	Black's, Md.
HON. FREDERICK STUMP,	Perryville, Md.
WILLIAM B. USILTON,	Chestertown, Md.
W. F. HINES, M. D.,	Chestertown, Md.
HON. JOHN W. CRISFIELD,	Princess Anne, Md.
CHAS. T. WESTCOTT, ESQ.,	Chestertown, Md.
HON. JOHN B. BROWN,	Centreville, Md.
W. M. SLAY, ESQ.,	Chestertown, Md.
HON. M. deK. SMITH,	Chestertown, Md.
H. W. VICKERS, ESQ.,	Chestertown, Md.
HON. W. R. MARTIN,	Easton, Md.
HIRAM M. BROWN,	Chestertown, Md.
HON. WM. D. BURCHINAL,	Chestertown, Md.
T. W. ELIASON,	Chestertown, Md.
R. D. HYNSON, ESQ.,	Chestertown, Md.
SAMUEL VANNORT,	Chestertown, Md.
G. B. WESTCOTT,	Chestertown, Md.
E. F. PERKINS, Treasurer,	Chestertown, Md.

CHARLES W. REID.

CHARLES W. REID, principal of Washington College, was born in Chester county, Pennsylvania. Both of his parents came from England. He completed the four years' course at the Philadelphia High School, after spending two years in the grammar schools. He entered the Junior Class of Dickinson College, where he graduated in the summer of '65, the honor man of his class.

He immediately organized a private school at Milford, Delaware, which he taught for two years. In the fall of '67, he went to Germany to study the classical languages. He spent one year at the University of Gottingen, one at Berlin, and six months at Bonn, mainly in the study of Greek.

During his absence in Europe, he travelled through Germany, France, Holland, Belgium, Italy and Sicily, and spent three months in Greece. On his return to America, he was elected a professor in Alleghany College, Meadville, Pa., where he filled the chair of modern languages for seven years, and that of Greek for eight. In 1886, he was appointed professor of Greek and German in St. John's College. In 1889, he was chosen Principal of Washington College.

Dr. C. W. Reid.

Faculty.

C. W. REID, A. M., PH. D., Principal.
    Professor of Greek, Mental, Moral and Political Science.

JAMES ROY MICOU, A. M., Vice-Principal.
    Professor of Latin Language and Literature.

CAROLINE PETTIGREW, Preceptress.
    Teacher of Modern Languages.

CAPT. JAMES I. STEVENS, B. Sc.,
    Professor of Natural Science.

J. S. W. JONES, A. M.,
    Professor of Mathematics.

EDWARD J. CLARKE, A. M.,
    Professor of English and Elocution.

ALVA B. BURRIS,
    Director of Gymnasium.

J. S. W. JONES, A. M.,
    Secretary.

E. J. CLARKE, A. M.,
    Librarian.

JAMES ROY MICOU.

JAMES ROY MICOU, vice-principal of this college and professor of Latin, was born in Essex county, Va., in 1859. After attending for nine years private schools in his native town, he was sent in his fifteenth year to Richmond, where he spent four years at one of the best schools in the State, its course of instruction being fully equal to that of the smaller colleges. Entering the University of Virginia in October, 1877, he graduated in the following June in the schools of Latin, German, French and Pure Mathematic, thereby accomplishing in one session about one-half of the A. M. course, which always requires three and often four or more years for its completion. Forced by circumstances to leave the university, he began the study of law, and was in due time admitted to the bar. He had, however, meanwhile, accepted the position of instructor in mathematics in McCabe's University School, Petersburg, Va., which position he held for six years, resigning to begin the practice of his profession. Before settling anywhere, he was elected vice-principal of this college, and bidding a final farewell to Coke and Blackistone, he in 1887 came to Washington College, where he has since remained.

Prof. James Roy Micou.

CLASS OF '95.

MOTTO: *Certum pete finem.*
COLORS: *Orange and Olive.*
YELL: *Halabaloo! Konick! Konick! Who's alive! '95! Bulldog!*

OFFICERS.

J. F. CAREY,	President.
G. E. WILLIAMSON,	Vice-President.
W. C. COPPER,	Secretary.
H. V. HOLLOWAY,	Treasurer.
N. CAMERON,	Historian.
H. G. SIMPERS,	Poet.
MAY L. MATTHEWS,	Prophetess.

MEMBERS.

BROWN, W. C.,	MERRIKEN, R.,
COMERON, N.,	NICHOLSON, R. J.,
CAREY, J. F.,	PERKINS, H.,
COPPER, W. C.,	SIMPERS, H. G.,
HOLLOWAY, H. V.,	VENABLES, W. F.,
MATTHEWS, MAY L.,	WILLIAMSON, G. E.

HISTORY

Alas! it has begun! Not the history, for the date of its beginning is unknown; but the writing of the history of the class of '95. Oh! how I should pity Freemen or Momnisen if they were the objects upon which a Senior editor might vent his wrath for their laziness and negligence (if they had any), as one has been doing for the past month upon the historian of our class.

At the present time our number is twelve, eleven gentlemen and one lady, this one representative of the fair sex being the first to graduate at Washington College.

Some have witnessed all the horrors and fears of Prepdom; some have first learned to "wield" the "brush" among the "freshies," and some have dropped down, on a cool September day, as if from some haven of knowledge, and wit never before heard from, and distinguished from other "Sophs" by their exceeding "Freshness," while others not a great number hailed us on our onward course from the Junior boat of knowledge, which had evidently become too learned or too "tough."

But at the same time, while some entered our ranks from other classes, still not a few have quit us, either on account of affairs which demanded their undivided attention in the lower classes or from a desire to better develop their faculties by seeking a broader field for their applications.

How many have dropped by the wayside is hard to tell; there are a few who, at one time boasting of the honor of being a member of our class, might be likened to a ship at anchor with the continuous current of '95's, '96's, '97's and '98's making up the stream and flowing by, leaving the unfortunates to the fate of adversity.

Behold the records of the class of '95! You will not have to look at the record books to see that this class excels all others, but look on the athletic records, the base-ball and foot-ball fields, the tennis court and every other kind of athletics, and you will behold great achievements accomplished by '95, which will be handed down to posterity.

In the demerit book we can justly claim the highest records. Yes, we are an unfortunate set of beings, to be compelled to suffer the pains, and to swallow the medicine intended for others.

We stand a bulwark of defence to the "Freshies" and "Sophs" in those hours when a "hundred" is staring them in the face or when "bay nags" cannot be had on this side of the Atlantic to alleviate the pressure on the brain.

I would tell you, my dear readers, how we combined with the "wise men" (?) wiped off the base-ball field the "Freshies" and (Juniors) in days to come, but I am not allowed to predict, so you can only surmise our victory. With an account of '95's ability I will not have to deviate from my promise and tell its possibilities as "Sufficient to the day is the evil thereof." Oh! posterity! attend my "companions in arms and brothers in peril," with success in all their undertakings ; teach them the way of politics and the rulings of history.

HISTORIAN.

Class Poem.

The goal is reached, the outstretched course is run,
The victor's meed is ours, and we have done
With all that dims the path of progress. Years
Seem days, and days seem seconds now that fears
Dissolved, have disappeared amid the accomplished record.
Henceforth time must have new meanings and afford
Perpetual triumph—ne'er dismay untoward.

So here we stand and mark the milestones past;
Recall the memories issuing first and last
From out the associations of these years;
Embrace the pleasant; shed a few, salt tears;
Smile at the recollections of our innocent days,—
Our adolescence, quaking, queer, and awkward ways,
That held us in suspense and failure fast.

What currents start with every back-look now!
Those dreaded shapes that, on beetling brow
Of high success were seen professors vast,
Have, in our new attainments, finally passed
Into the realm of men. And we ourselves, transformed
By reaches into learning, sped unharmed
Into their noble semblance—men at last!

So Juniors, Sophs, and you ye Freshmen small,
Look up, take heart, be not in dastard thrall
Unto the "Impossible!" Scorn that coward word
That we have put to flight! And by us pattern
If on the sweets of learning ye would fatten.
What we have done, perhaps ye, too, may do;
Screw up your courage! dare be true
Unto the example handed down to you!

Perkins, Holloway, Copper, Cameron,
Williamson, Nicholson, Matthews, Cary,
Brown. Sanpers, Merriken.

SENIOR CLASS.

But with this parting word of solemn admonition,
Comes o'er us all, a feeling like contrition
For what is vanished. Have we shorn the lock
Of Samson strength, and is it the Future mocks,
Like some Delilah, at our untried power?
Do "sheepskins" carry in them all we need?
Will absence from these halls an ignorance breed?
Say, fellows, darkening o'er us lower
Some vengeful fate, unless we make our hour,
And by inherent vigor "take the lead."

What then of sadness comes with our reflections
That college days are past, and the sweet recollections
Of chum and class-mates all subside with time,
This e'er abides: No change of fortune, clime,
Or any other circumstance can spoil the truth
Infixed into our hearts! Time's gnawing tooth,
Nor all that beats upon us, can our souls despoil.
We act in lofty spheres. The Holy Grail
Called forth no higher ardor than we yield in toil
For truth; and by and in that sign
We "live, move, have our being," in fine.

Come then, and fill the beaker to the brim,
And quaff the strength of reason's joy! No sin
Lies in such action. And may propitious days
Still measure to the needs of learning's ways.
Professors, students, and tender "preps,"
Good fortune 'tend you! May your steps
Like giant paces move toward the unseen
Where God stands regnant! As for us I ween
No higher blessedness than this is near—
To do the right untrammeled, without fear.

PROPHECY.

"ALL'S WELL THAT ENDS WELL."

Webster defines prophecy as a declaration of something to come. As God only knows future events with certainty, no being but God, or some person informed by Him, can utter a REAL prophecy.

So, my classmates, if Fate should have better things in store for you than my mind alone dictates, remember I do not claim to be a REAL seer nor yet a "gypsy fortune teller."

"Coming events cast their shadows before," and however illy defined those shadows may be, upon them only can the human mind depend in order to foretell with the least degree of certainty the workings of fate.

I was sitting one evening in the wood and "twilight gray had in her sober livery all things clad; silence accompanied," and my thoughts reverted to my school-days now almost over; each of my classmates were in turn presented to my mind and his face and characteristics impressed upon my memory. Realizing the fact that soon the parting must come and each pursue the path which destiny had marked out for him, I could not refrain from exclaiming aloud—would that I might know something of each one's future!

No sooner had the words escaped my lips when at my side a diminutive form appeared which I at once recognized as a fairy of the wood; a voice like sweetest music fell upon my ear; imagine my astonishment at the following words—"My child, your wish shall be gratified. With my magic wand will I bestow upon you the gift of prophecy, a scene in the life of each will be presented to you, and what now you know not, shall be made clear unto you," and gently touching me with her tiny wand she disappeared in the twilight.

For the moment my bewildered mind could scarcely comprehend what had passed, but when the intelligence flashed upon me that I had been endowed with a most wonderful gift, a feeling of ineffable joy took possession of me. I felt myself transported, the scene of the wood slowly receded from my view, and in its place came a busy metropolis; years, too, seemed to have passed over my head, the twentieth century had just dawned. Closer observation proved the city to be one renowned in history, Boston.

'Tis not strange that this port presented greater attractions for Mr. Brown than all others, for in days gone by that name held a peculiar fascination for him. But " Love's young dream " is past, and his highest hope is realized—the title " Prof. Brown," bestowed upon him as a nickname in his college days, has become a reality, he now holds the honored position of Prof. of Science in Boston University and his beautiful home is presided over by —— ah! well, we all know whom. Long life and happiness to Prof. Brown.

1900. Our valedictorian was proficient alike in Greek and Latin, and was always happiest when conjugating a Greek verb, or studying the thousand and one Latin rules (and as many exceptions) in obedience to the eleventh commandment—"Thou shalt know thy Latin Grammar from cover to cover." As tutor at his Alma Mater, Mr. Cameron has adopted this same commandment as his own, and woe be unto the " Preplet " who fails to remember a rule thereof. At the moment this scene is presented to me, he is instructing a class in Bellum Helvetium; notwithstanding his mischievous propensities of bygone days, Mr. Cameron has developed into a tutor of the first order, well calculated to inspire the "Senior Preps" with awe.

1905. The next scene lies in New York. An observer on —————— street cannot fail to be attracted by a mammoth stone structure, over whose massive doors appears the name of the firm

J. A. F. CAREY & CO., Publishers.
School Books a Specialty.

This firm has supplanted that well-known one of A————s & Co., and keeps on hand a first-class stock of Latin, German and Greek ponies. Mr. Carey, having learned from experience that equestrian exercise is a healthful recreation, heartily recommends it to his patrons, and so fulfills the golden rule—Sell ponies unto others as you have had them sold to you.

1912. As the college buildings are lost in the distance, the landscape becomes dotted with thrifty and pretty farm houses. The most noticeable of these is an almost palatial residence, the sloping lawn with its stately trees, birds flitting from bough to bough, and fountains playing in the sunshine, present a scene so like fairyland—I am speechless with delight. In the foreground a gentleman is standing, whose countenance plainly says,—" I am monarch of all I survey." Though old Father Time has wrought some changes in this one, he has not succeeded in wholly effacing the familiar lines,—the name graven on memory's page can be no other than W. C. Copper.

1918. The Legislative Hall of our nation presents a scene of peculiar interest ; a bill has been introduced in the Senate claiming the right of suffrage for the women of Delaware. Senator Holloway has just risen to speak ; his eloquence is well attested by the way he holds the undivided attention of his colleagues. He is one of the ablest defenders of the cause, and if earnestness on his part will insure its success the issue is not doubtful. A faint echo of his closing words come to me—" When the women of America take the platforms and the ballot boxes, and not until then, will we have a government of the people, by the people and for the people."

1916. I am somewhat startled at seeing a feminine form; why yes, to be sure, it is the girl graduate, May Matthews. Her countenance, manner and bearing confirm my suspicion that she is a spinster. Though having had an unusual number of opportunities to enter into connubial bliss (what spinster has not?), she decided her mission was better fulfilled alone. Her errand seems to be philanthropic as she wends her way through the by-streets and alleys with her basket filled with viands, flowers and a goodly array of temperance tracts. The little street urchin hails her as his friend, for well he knows sundry cakes and cookies will find their way to his begrimed hands.

We wish her "bon-heur" in her chosen mission.

1901. In college days a certain classmate's susceptibility to Cupid's dart was favorable to early nuptials, and in this the omens were not mistaken. A pretty cottage among the flowers and trees proclaims the fact that it is just built for two; there appears at the door a sweet-faced lady who must certainly be the mistress of the house. Suddenly my attention is drawn by a familiar whistle, "Listen to the Mocking bird," ah! that explains it all, this can be the home of none other than Mr. Merriken. As pastor of a pretty village church, he is happy in the love and respect accorded him by his fellowmen.

1902. As the last vision takes its departure, the spacious halls of Harvard University become clearly defined. The galleries are thonged with visitors; commencement exercises are in progress and the valedictorian advances. His eloquence, commanding presence and grace of gesture attest him a born orator. The audience gazes at him with rapt attention, and when he makes his closing remarks the fragrance of flowers mingles with applause, loud and long. His face is certainly familiar, but memory fails to recall the name; curiously, I glance at the program nearest me and read— R. J. Nicholson.

1915. Mr. Perkins' antagonism to the co-educational system prompts me to some little indulgence of imagination as a preliminary to the scene. Perhaps, after the lapse of time some "sweet girl grad" of his Alma Mater has overcome his aversion, but my mind pictures him of the same opinion still. We shall see! Ah, my gift does not fail me; a paragraph in one of the leading journals presents itself.—"An item of interest reaches us from the Fiji Islands. Mr. H. E. Perkins, a graduate of Washington College, and an earnest worker in school reform, some years ago directed his footsteps to these islands, where an unusually broad field of action awaited him. Here, after surviving the cannibalistic tendencies of the natives, and working zealously with the missionaries for a period of five years, he succeeded in establishing a school, where the heathen boys and girls are given no opportunity for the exchanging of languishing glances and surreptitious notes." Let us wish him success in his undertaking.

1908. The present scene is not unlike the last, in the fact that it, too, takes place in a distant country. Surely, that figure resting there under a tree is a familiar one! Yes, as he turns, 'tis easy to recognize another member of '95. But let me glance at the newspaper he has just scornfully thrown aside. This passage meets my eye (suffice to say, it is a Democratic paper),—"The report comes to us that Mr. H. G. Simpers, in his tour around the world, has reached Africa, where he intends to remain for sometime, with the ostensible purpose of encouraging among the

Prof. J. I. Stephens.

natives emigration to the United States, a majority of Republican votes being in demand."

1908. New York. 'Tis the Patriarch's ball—Conservatory, sequestered nook. A couple seated therein, the belle of the ball and—"mirabile dictu"—our old classmate W. F. Venables!!! The pleading depicted upon his countenance would assure the observer that truly, 'tis that sweet story of old which is being so earnestly repeated. Who would have thought that Cupid would choose this one of our number for his target! As the happy guests pass to and fro, he remains seemingly oblivious to all surroundings. The scene recalls to my mind those lines of Emerson,—" The world uncertain comes and goes, the lover rooted stays."

1930. " Oft ye have heard the Scriptures rehearse, ' the first shall be last, and the last shall be first.' " Was it not said, that all the virtues of the Senior Class were combined in this one? Then, certainly he must be first. One of his classmates, thinking he was paying him the highest tribute possible, said,—" If he was a 'gal,' I'd marry him." Looking in through the windows of a large building in the city of ——— ———, we are reminded that there is sickness and suffering in this wide world of ours. Moving from cot to cot, we notice a gray-haired gentleman, whose cheering words and gentle touch act as a balm to the sick. Dr. Williamson is fulfilling a noble destiny, which will procure for him a starry crown in that bright realm, where there is no suffering, no death.

Class of '96.

Motto:—*In Omnia Paratus.*
Colors and Yell: Rickety Rix! Rickety Rix!
Behold the Class of '96!
Rally ha-roo,
How do you do?
All is well with the Lemon and Blue.

OFFICERS.

Edward M. Noble,	President.
M. Belle Boston,	Vice-President.
Charles W. Easley.	Secretary.
E. Rigby McDorman,	Treasurer.
H. Arringdale Jump,	Historian.
Samuel R. Douglas,	Poet.

—ROLL.—

B, that's Miss Boston, so pretty is she,
Much liked by the Washington College " B."

B is Miss Burchinal, a fine young maid,
She, with no fellow would not make a trade,
So quiet is she, as gentle as a lamb,
But, occasionally she smiles on our big " Sam."

D, that's Douglas, the "Junior class Puck,"
    The clown in the circus he certainly can mock,
    As well as talk a girl from her frock ;
    He's loving, he sings, his superiors are few,
    But the funniest of all he wears an eight shoe.

E, that's Easley, who is pretty and spunky,
    The greatest orator from the noted Kentucky,
    He studies at noon and evening as well,
    The weight of his brain no one can tell.

G stands for Glover, the college half-back,
    Who rides sometimes on a pony's bareback,
    He's quiet and timid, but whiskers can grow,
    I'll tell you just now or else you wont know.

J is for Jump and Jack-in-pot too,
    Who does all his walking in No. 1 shoes,
    He's jolly and jovial and has lots of fun,
    And goes to bed early when day's work is done.

M is McDorman, the young Irish lad,
    A sweet sixteener, and often quite bad ;
    He plays and sings, and reads of the system,
    A doctor he'll be, no doubt of that question.

N is Noble, the great mathematician,
    In summer he loafs or else goes a-fishing,
    He views all the stars through the great telescope,
    But talks as slow as an old-fashioned poke.

U is Usilton, the base-ball twirler,
    Who's struck on a lady, but cannot court her.

HISTORY.

Realizing it as a great privilege to be historian of '96, and with a true sense of our inability, we attempt to champion the cause of this illustrious and renowned class. There have been many societies, organizations, and Junior Classes in the history of Washington College, but never has a class become so widely known, so justly famed, and so highly honored as the class of '96. When we look back over the past,—and when we say the past, we mean our past, and not that of any other class, for some of them have none—we see that the class of '96 did not spring from the race of the immortal gods, nor did its existence begin when the shutters were silently spirited away from the West Hall. No; a thousand times, no! The class of '96 entered upon the four years' course, and we all matriculated. Our record as a class has been one of which we can be justly proud, and one which other classes envy. Judging from the industry and ability of the class of '96 during its college career, one might predict its future greatness and prosperity ; but since it is not in our province to prophesy, but simply to state facts, we will refrain from foretelling its future. All through its college course, the class of '96 has been a quiet, unassuming and modest class. It has no need to have its glorious and world-renowned deeds enrolled upon the pages of history, since they are so indelibly stamped upon the memories of their fellow-students, that they can never be effaced.

During the latter part of the Freshman year, we engaged in that fascinating and useful study—Botany. In the beautiful afternoons, when we fain would seek some shady nook and while away the pleasant hours, forgetful of to-morrow's lesson, we were compelled to travel over new-plowed fields, and along the highways and hedges, in search of those sweet-scented wild flowers, for the purpose of analysis. But the Freshman year is a thing of the past, yet fond recollection presents to our view the orchard, the meadow, the wide-spreading mill-pond, and every loved spot where we were accustomed to seek flowers. Our Sophomore year was a very quiet one, and devoted mostly to our studies, in which we were victorious in the end. The Junior year has been the busiest, the most interesting and important. The latter part of the year has been mostly occupied in the publication of our Annual, which we modestly believe will be a success. On the foot-ball field, two of our members hold up the honors of our class; while on the diamond we have no representative, though not from lack of ability, but merely indifference. If history repeats itself, the future of the class of '96 can be safely predicted as the most prosperous, peaceable, happy and brilliant. There has always been displayed a unanimity of feeling concerning all class matters, and after three years of substantial college work, good fellowship and a record of which we are proud, leave to our reader a history which we trust may interest those who come after us. It is with sincere regret, that we learn that some of us, perhaps, will not return; but we shall ever cherish the memories of the past, confident in the belief that we carry with us the best wishes of all.

HISTORIAN.

Class Poem.

Brave knights and maidens fair, we are
    Just entering on a private strife.
To stamp our fame upon the stars
    And be the best throughout our life.

While traveling on this path begun,
    Broad fields appear before our eyes,
We see new triumphs to be won
    To write our fame upon the skies.

'Tis true, our path's not strewn with flow'rs;
    But noble valor, strength of brain,
Will urge us to our utmost pow'rs
    To win the heights which we'd attain.

And now we say come weal, come woe,
    Be guilty of no laggard's crime.
Let's pluck the fruits that always grow
    Upon the banks, O stream of Time!

Our compliments, tho' from the heart,
    Can on thee no more vanity fix,
For that has been the largest part
    Of thee, O class of ninety-six!

Prof. J. S. W. Jones.

Class of '97.

Motto: *Virtute non Verbis.*
Colors: *Orange and Blue.*
Yell: *Hurrah, Hurrah, Hurrah Ree! '97, '97, W. C.*

OFFICERS.

Wm. E. S. Thomas,	President.
Ernest Cruikshank,	Vice-President.
Edward F. Webb,	Rec. Secretary.
Geo. C. Graham, Jr.,	Cor. Secretary.
W. E. Burke Faithful,	Treasurer.
T. Howard Fowler,	Historian.
Spencer M. Hurtt,	Poet.

MEMBERS.

Brinsfield, D.,	Graham, G. C., Jr.,
Covey, A. H.,	Hurtt, S. M.,
Coulbourne, J. L.,	Massey, T.,
Cruikshank, E.,	Quillen, S. M., Jr.,
Faithful, W. E. B.,	Thomas, W. E. S.,
Fowler, T. H.,	Webb, E. F.

HISTORY.

The class of '97! What a world of meaning lies hidden in these four unpretentious words. Words unassuming, like the members of this class, who, although they feel their importance and realize that they are regarded by their fellow students as bright lights of the ninteenth century, still are modest and not puffed up with vanity. In our days of Prepdom, it was early recognized that we were destined for great things. In our Freshman year, the number of "square hundreds knocked out" was something remarkable, especially in that branch known as zoology, or as the Preps used to call it, "Science of cats," because we made such an exhaustive and pleasant study of that noble animal. But it is in this, our Sophomore year, that we have attained our "summum bonum."

It is a striking characteristic of this class, and one which plainly shows that they are brainy, that the longer the lessons given us, the better they are prepared. This year our record is wonderful. In chemistry, often have we been nearly blown up by our habit of inquiring into the very wherefore of everything. In languages, we have attained that degree of excellence, that sometimes becoming tired of English, we converse with each other in Latin, Greek, or French, with such astonishing ease that we have heard it said, that the professors of languages will soon resign, being unable to teach us more. In the field we are excellent. Although we have only one member of our class on the base-ball team, still his playing is such that he is conceded by all to be well worthy of the class of '97. How gracefully does he walk out upon the field, and how politely and with what a sweet smile does he doff his cap when cheered by the ladies, as he invariably is. Several other positions on the team might be filled by '97, but being modest, we do not think it just to take more than our share.

One thing that puzzles all the boys is how that class of '97 does get right there with the ladies, though we are sure that this should not puzzle them when they consider our personal appearance. But we are modest and don't like to speak of that. The most powerful secret of our success, excluding of course our good looks, is that we are not backed down by trifles. For instance, a '97 goes to church, sees a young lady with whom he desires to walk home. Somebody steals his hat. Does this stop him? No, sir! He asks her to wait for him, and after half an hour's search finds it and walks off smiling with the young lady on his arm, leaving the fellow waiting on the church steps, feeling rather "hoodooed."

As I lift the shadowy veil and peer into the dim future, I see before me all of old '97 holding high positions, as had been predicted. There's our "Modern Daniel Webster" of Caroline, holding the Senate spellbound by his eloquence. Here is our dignified "Father" of Talbot, always so distinguished in debate, now Archbishop and, yes, he still has his hair "a la pompadour." And all the others I see before me, fulfilling the expectation of my early prophecy. Noble ambition!

I would then, give advice to those following us: Go to the class of '97 for instruction; consider her ways and be wise; follow in her footsteps and know that "nothing great is lightly won" (except by '97). And so we go on doing all things well, and

> Still the world wonders more and more,
> At the powerful big train of the Sophomore ;
> And it is certain, and all agree,
> That we are *the* class of W. C.

HISTORIAN.

Class Poem.

Our fond *Alma Mater*,
   In ninety and seven,
Will enrich with its honors
   Our illustrious 'leven.

Two years now have past,
   Two years yet remain;
The ladder half mounted
   Till its summit we gain.

Virtute non verbis,
   Our maxim we read;
'Tis power in valor,
   'Tis courage we need.

Our pennant is orange
   With the clear heaven's blue,
Which has for its symbol,
   The good and the true.

The class-room gives labors
   Of Herculean size,
The victory is ours,
   Our honors, the prize.

We have won Cæsar's battles,
   We've laid Livy aside;
And now 'tis with Cicero,
   Rome's orator and pride.

Though Greek may be Grecian,
   Yet we fail to comprehend
Why the class of eleven,
   May not submit it to bend.

The lands we have trodden,
   The fields we have chained ;
The bearings well taken
   With their angles contained.

We *parley* in *Francais*
   With marked Parisian case ;
In the Greek and the Latin
   Our words but seldom please.

In words of burning eloquence,
   We boast our mother tongue,
The greatest, grandest language,
   Our own ! from Saxon sprung.

The chemist's lore and symbol
   Have given to past time thought,
How nature's art and science
   In fixed truth are wrought.

With brightest hopes and courage
   May truth and wisdom blend,
To guide our mental efforts
   Till school days reach their end.

Farewell ! we bid you Seniors,
   Loved school days' course is run :
Life's battles now confront you,
   God's will, not ours, be done.

IN MEMORIAM.

JAMES D. COWMAN,

CLASS OF '97.

DIED AUGUST 18, 1894.

Class of '98.

MOTTO: *Haud palma sine pulvere.*
COLORS: *Old Rose and Black.*
YELL: *Ray! Rah! Ree!*
Ray! Rah! Ree!
Class of '98 W. C.

OFFICERS.

LEON A. DAVIS,	President.
HORACE M. BECK,	Vice-President.
NORMAN S. DUDLEY,	Rec. Secretary.
H. FOSTER PERKINS,	Cor. Secretary.
HARRY RICKEY,	Treasurer.
JOHN W. WHARTON,	Historian.
AMY RUSSELL,	Poetess.

MEMBERS.

BECK, H. M.,	RUSSELL, A.,
DAVIS, L. A.,	STAM, ANNIE,
DOWNEY, C.,	STAM, LOUISE,
DUDLEY, N. S.,	SHERWOOD, W. N.,
JACKSON, W. E.,	SMITH, M. DEK., JR.,
MCCABE, A. J.,	TOULSON, J.,
MCCABE, E. H., JR.,	VICKERS, G.,
PARDEE, J. S. E.,	VICKERS, JR., H. W.,
PATTON, M.,	WESTCOTT, M.,
PERKINS, H. F.,	WHALAND, G.,
RICHARDS, J. A.,	WHARTON, J. W.,
RICKEY, H.,	WHITE, J. M.

HISTORY.

It is a herculean task to record in small compass the achievements of the class of '98. Volumes might be written about it, and yet the half would not be told. In the first place, never have we felt the full import of our motto, "haud palma sine pulvere," as we do in our present undertaking, when the history of our class is to appear for the first time, amid her sister classes before the public.

Observe that young man who was one year ago an awkward country boy, is now on the highway to fame, as he is already an excellent speaker and logical debater. What is it that has given him this readiness of speech and acuteness of perception? How is it that he is so conversant with the ways of men? What is it that gave to him the power of being so readily the master of the situation under all circumstances? Ah, my friend, could the veil be lifted for a year from that class, where between young men and women a great, though friendly, rivalry for leadership has been going on, where diamond has cut diamond until all the imperfections have been removed, then would you understand the change; but as it is, we can only say that being members of the class of '98, has developed them into paragons of manly and womanly excellence.

Taking our class as a whole, we feel that we can say without fear of successful contradiction that the college has never, in the long chain of its history, had a stronger link than our class. It never had a class superior to this in refinement, industry and culture. They are from homes crowned with taste and worth, the sons and daughters of parents who excel in the virtues and accomplishments of society, and who teach them the value and merit of mental as well as bodily adornment; who point the way to higher pleasures and sweeter joys than those that pertain to the gratification of the coarser senses of physical life. There is so much implied

Prof. E. J. Clarke.

in the beautiful sentiment of the poet, "My mind to me a kingdom is." Mental possessions are of greatest value, and we commend as well as compliment our members in their earnest pursuit. The question which at present most concerns them is that of education. It has been and is discussed in the rooms, halls, and, even now, on the campus. And why? Because, upon the education of themselves depends the foundation of their future success and prosperity. The past we know ; the present we have with us, and the future is assured, for "where there's a will, there's always a way." "In the beginning, God said let there be light and there was light." In the beginning of our course at college we said, "Let there be toil and there was toil." We have set an example for those who come after us, who may look to the Freshman class of '95 for a guide, an example worthy to be followed. Our readers, we know, have the assurance that they will find such an example in us. May those classes that follow us walk in our footsteps, "and advancing, leave behind them" a bright and beautiful memory, which, like ours, can never fade.

Our range of information is very remarkable. Where is the person who dares deny that the standard of scholarship in our class is unprecedented in the history of the college? In our class may be found classical, scientific and mathematical students, and oratorical as well. It is not surprising that before this array of geniuses the reader stands appalled. But our ability is by no means entirely intellectual. In athletics, too, we are well represented. The football team last fall would have been but a negative quantity without some members, who, at the risk of life and limb, by their brilliant playing added greater glory to the class of '98.

Again, in base-ball this spring, some of the very important positions were filled by Freshmen. '98 to-day has more than a score of members; yet with open palm and voice ringing with welcome, we say to all that have an honest, conscientious purpose at heart, "Come, ye ends of the earth, and we will do you good." There is ever a vacant chair in '98 awaiting to receive the forlorn, tear-stained and homesick student when he arrives at Washington College; and although we cannot bring to him his mother, nor allow him to meet his JULIET so frequently as was his want, yet we will admit him into the presence of the king of all MYSTIC four-footed beasts, upon which he may ride into other "vales of happiness," thereby constraining him to form new ties, assume new obligations, and by the corner-stone of a character noble, virtuous and charitable. Every member that enters the class needs our help; and we are anxious to assist him, feeling conscious that in due time he will be enabled to stand alone, and in turn constitute a pillar for others to lean against for support. It is needless to say that in such a large body of young women and men, the qualities of the individual, whether good or evil, cannot long be kept secret from his associates, and true worth will ever shine, though its lustre be dimmed by the cloud of circumstance. Further, I may add, that as the marble from the quarry becomes the polished shaft by its contact with other equally hard substances, so our members, by elbowing one another, reap a far greater reward in the class, and, at the close of their active career in '98's class, go forth into the world as intellectual phenomena to grace the varied walks of life.

I will not go further. The subject, as has been said, is inexhaustible. We are an eminently SELECT class, and advocate as our theory, "Quality and not quantity." All who know us will certify to the truth of the statement that the quality is unexceptionable.

Class Poem.

Sauntering up the board-walk,
  We near the echoing halls,
Where germs of wisdom nestle
  Within their massive walls.

Of all the college classes,
  Name a better if you can;
The one we all love best
  Is the Freshman in the van.

It has a score of members,
  Both lads and lasses fair;
On week days you can see them
  Conning Latin with care.

Botany gives us joy in study,
  Mathematics just as well,
How much our French enchants us
  'Tis very hard to tell.

As the school-room, so in life,
  So many things perplex;
In Rhetoric we alter
  Our language most complex.

We have a worthy leader,
  By no one is he passed,
He's been so very faithful
  And will be to the last.

We give our members nicknames,
  I'll mention one if you please,
He boasts of talent and of wit,
  The noble "Socrates."

Three years must yet go gliding by
   When these dear friends will separate ;
But may they ne'er forget
   The class of '98.

Our teachers we will not forget,
   May the seeds their hands have sown
Yield rich and varied harvests,
   Which they will proudly own.

We must bid our last adieus
   And o'er life's threshold pass,
With a stern unyielding master,
   No more a loving class.

Should we not meet on earth again,
   When the trials of life are past,
May we wear bright crowns of bliss
   In Paradise at last.

There will be no parting then
   In that bright world untold.
May all of my classmates dear
   Be gathered in the fold.

PREPARATORY DEPARTMENT.

A Prep Thought.

A dreamy little preplet tucked his corpus in his cot,
Put aside his daily griefs, and thought, and thought and thought.

Thought of birdie in the tree-tops, thought of spring and flowers and love;
Aye, it was a spoony—that dream of his turtle dove.

Thought if the "beginnin" was as Seniors said, alive,
He would stay and hear the "lordies" give their yell for ninety-five.

Thought he'd eat his hat to know, how 'neath the sun it haps
Those Seniors seem so lordly—such blamed hard-headed chaps.

Thought of that man Holloway who calls the club his own;
Thought of "Browney," who, he'd heard, is never seen alone;

Thought of "Simp" and Perkins, Copper, "Dick," and many more,—
Thought and thought and thought until his head was sore.

Thought—this timid preplet—he'd be blowed if he had knowledge
What such startlin' fools was doin' round a college.

Saint nor Solomon—this preplet—but he thought he knew a few.
Thought he and never doubted, as some men will do.
Thus it happened, that this preplet lying on his cot of straw,
Thought a rustlin' kick was proper in fate's case-hardened maw.

Thus it happened, as I told you, to this little prep of ours,
He who thought and never doubted, thought until the sunny hours.

MISS PETTIGREW, *Preceptress.*

Preparatory Department.

THIRD YEAR.

Anthony, Harry
Anderson, J. S.
Barnes, J. U.
Beck, Sallie
Blackiston, M.
Boston, C. D.
Brown, S. C.
Burris, A. B.
Cooper, S. T.
Coursey, S. C.
Culp, Susie B.
Frazier, Rose

Janvier, E. G.
Longfellow, E. W.
Longfellow, Ellyn
McFeely, George
Murray, Lucy
Nicholson, H. B.
Simpers, Frank
Ward, V. F.
Watts, G. A.
Wilkins, Noland
Wilkins, Olivia

SECOND YEAR.

Brice, M.
Brown, H. S.
Copper, Minnie
Dashiell, B. H.
Eliason, Holt
Eliason, John
Hines, Frank

Lucas, Eugene
Rogers, Marian
Simpers, Raymond
Stam, Rudolph
Toulson, Hallie
Thompson, Claudia

FIRST YEAR.

ELIASON, IRMA
PERKINS, ETHEL

SMITH, ANNIE
VICKERS, CLARA

W. G. Idyl.

THE PREP THAT WEARS A SUNNY SMILE.

I know a little preplet maid
  With the softest, sweetest smile,
As though her silly little head
  Upheld a Senior tile.

Her voice, the dearest little coo,
  Her eyes are bottled stars;
Her footfalls soft as even's dew,
  Venusian form she bears.

Her very presence seemeth bliss,
  Her heart is full of lore,
And though I love the maid no less,
  I worship knowledge more.

LITERARY SOCIETIES.

Mt. Vernon Literary Society.

Wie die Arbeit so der Lohn.

1847-1895.

PRESIDENTS OF THE SOCIETY FOR 1894-1895.

FIRST TERM:

EDWARD M. NOBLE,

Denton.

SECOND TERM:

WM. F. VENABLES,

Mardela.

MT. VERNON LITERARY SOCIETY.

Mt. Vernon.

OFFICERS.

WM. F. VENABLES. . . . . President.
NORMAN CAMERON. . . . . . . Vice-President.
L. A. DAVIS. . . . . Rec. Sec'y.
GEORGE C. GRAHAM, JR., . . . Cor. Sec'y.
J. I. COULBOURNE. . . . . Treasurer.

MEMBERS.

BARNES, J. U.	JACKSON, W. E.
BOSTON, C. D.	LONGFELLOW, E.
BROWN, H.	NOBLE, E. M.
BURRIS, A. V.	PATTON, M.
CAMERON, N.	PARDEE, J. E.
COVEY, A. H.	QUILLEN, S. M., JR.
COULBOURNE, J. I.	STAM, R.
CRUIKSHANK, E.	THOMAS, W. E. S.
DAVIS, L. A.	VENABLES, W. F.
DUDLEY, N. S.	WEBB, E. F.
GRAHAM, G. C., JR.	ZEARFOSS, D. W. T.

SKETCH.

As the historian of the society sat listening to one of the white-haired founders of Mount Vernon, telling of "ye olden times," he thought of how much the story of Washington, as told in these pages, would be deprived; how much it would be like a crown robbed of its brightest jewel, if the history of the oldest literary society of Maryland was not linked with that of the institution to whose glory it contributes. And so I would ask you, kind reader, to look back with me, through nearly a half-century, at the happiest recollections of "Washington boys," now scattered far and wide.

It has been more than forty-eight years since the first class formed, at the reconstructed college, in their Sophomore year, the society that, through so many years and so many vicissitudes, has grown and flourished, sending forth the men whose success has given prominence to the superior source from which they received their training. As each year has brought its re-enforcement of recruits to swell the college ranks, they have been initiated into the mysteries of society life, and have taken up the welcome burden it imposes. It would be impossible to record here the long list of achievements that make our past so bright; the many obstacles that we have met and overcome, sometimes when we were almost crushed ourselves. It would be but telling an old story over and over again, with slight changes of persons and events, to recount these ups and downs that fill the life of a society, as they do those of men.

More than once the society has been shaken to the very foundation in the struggle for the most coveted honor to be obtained at Washington—the long term presidency of Mount

Vernon ; but the society has survived, and soared upward from the very jaws of destruction, a phœnix in all except name.

But the society has not always been compelled to contend with outside influences alone. Within her own halls, the struggle has more than once been fierce and bitter, leaving the society rent and torn. It was such a struggle as this, in which a second society had its birth, that gave the Philomathean Society to Washington College. Feeling aggrieved at what they considered unfair treatment, about fifteen members left our halls forever, and ere long the Philomathean Society was formed. We cannot but feel sorry at being deprived of these members, but now we see the benefit of two rival societies, if conducted without enmity. The Mount Vernon of to-day bears nothing but kindly regard for the offspring that owes so much of its success to the fostering care that the mother bestowed upon its founders in their early college days. Again, within the past year, the walls of Mount Vernon have echoed the fierce struggle's din, and seen other members pass without the portals that had received them so kindly in peaceful days gone by. Our laws have been put to the severest test, but constitutional right prevailed superior to the ambition of any of our members.

The fact that the work which the society offers for its members to perform differs little from the plan adopted more than forty years ago, testifies, as does its history, to the wisdom that gave Mount Vernon being, and guided its early halting steps into paths that now stretch far behind us. In its earliest days the members were divided into three classes, declaimers, essayists, and debaters, who alternated regularly each Saturday night. This order continued for two score years, and even for several years after the adoption of the new constitution, twelve years ago. But impromptu addresses have replaced compositions, and latterly, that the advantages that Mount Vernon confers may rank with its age, orations have been added to its line of work. Such is the training with which our beloved society seeks to make her members men in the fullest sense of the word. Not alone in an intellectual sense does our society raise its members to the peers of any, but in the name so dear to our hearts, we are carried back to that quiet spot where the Potomac ripples up to caress Virginia's historic shores, almost into the presence of him, who has hallowed the place, and are bidden to emulate the example of his pure manhood, and taught what true patriotism means, and what American boys can be. And as each year ushers in his natal day, the society does especial reverence to the name of Washington in their annual celebration, when the invited orators, inspired by the occasion and the presence of visitors and members, tell the responsibilities and realities of our citizenship. This celebration is an institution of the college, originated by and wholly devolving upon Mount Vernon. The first account we have of its observance, is a printed copy of the "address delivered before the Mount Vernon Society of Washington College by Edward A. Moore, Esq., February 22, 1853." The society also adds to the pleasures of Commencement Week by its anniversary exercises.

There is but a little more to tell. Mount Vernon stands, pointing with one hand to its record, enshrined upon memory's pages, and with the other, to the achievements of the future, offering, as a pledge for the fulfillment of her bright prospects, the glorious past, and promising that, imbued by the spirit handed down through fifty years, her members will ever strive to make her, as in the past, the glittering crown of Washington.

O, glorious, grand Mount Vernon! In thee are linked the present and the past; in thy bosom be enshrined the memory of years long passed, the hopes and expectations yet to be; gray-haired men are happy to claim thee for their own; young men who are yet to take their place in the great world, are proud to swell thy rolls! No words of mine can add to thy fame—thou speakest for thyself. A SON OF MOUNT VERNON.

Philomathean Literary Society.

Captate Occasionem.

1892--1895.

PRESIDENTS
For 1894-95.

FIRST TERM:

R. J. NICHOLSON.

SECOND TERM:

W. C. BROWN.

R. L. GLOVER,	Vice-President.
J. M. WHYTE,	Rec. Sec'y.
S. C. COURSEY,	Cor. Sec'y.
S. R. DOUGLAS,	Treasurer.
E. R. McDORMAN,	Chaplain.
C. W. EASLEY,	Asst. Chaplain.
A. J. McCABE,	Sergeant-at-arms.

PHILOMATHEAN LITERARY SOCIETY.

Philomathean.

COLORS: CREAM AND OLIVE.

MEMBERS.

Brown, W. C.	Kentucky.
Copper, W. C.	Florida.
Coursey, S. C.	Mississippi.
Dashiell, B. H.	Vermont.
Douglas, S. R.	Virginia.
Easley, C. W.	Maryland.
Faithful, W. E. B.	Alabama.
Glover, R. L.	Tennessee.
Holloway, H. V.	Illinois.
McCabe, A. J.	Delaware.
McCabe, E. H., Jr.	Texas.
McDorman, E. R.	New York.
Merriken, R.	Washington.
Nicholson, R. J.	California.
Richards, J. A.	Pennsylvania.
Ward, V. F.	Missouri.
Whyte, J. M.	Georgia.

SKETCH.

The Philomathean Society was organized in the collegiate year 1891-92, and held its first meeting on January 23d of that year. It began its prosperous career with a roll of fifteen active members, several of whom had withdrawn from the Mt. Vernon Society, because of some trouble in the annual election of officers. The latter, feeling that their rights as active members had not been duly respected by the old society, and seeing the need of another society to arouse interest in literary work which was fast dying out from lack of incentive, determined to form a new organization, and, if possible, to revive the spirit by entering into a kind of competition with their former brothers. At the first meeting, the following officers were elected: A. M. Hanna, '93, president; W. A. Melvin, '95, vice-president; H. V. Holloway, '95, recording secretary; R. L. Glover, '96, corresponding secretary; E. B. Polk, '94, treasurer; W. E. Bullock, '96, chaplain; F. B. Watts, '96, sergeant-at-arms. Under the direction of Mr. Hanna the society flourished, and, as had been the object of its organization, it aroused a literary enthusiasm, the like of which had never been manifested before in the history of the college. It gave its first public entertainment on the anniversary of the college, in May, 1893, in the form of a roaring farce. The success with which it was crowned, proved the ability of those who took part, and as the characters were all active members of the society, it showed that the Philomatheans had their share of the college talent. It has given a banquet each year, at which the Faculty and some intimate friends of the society have been present. These occasions have been enlivened with toasts by the members of the Faculty and by the students. The last one was especially interesting and enjoyable, owing to the presence of the members of our sister society, the Pieria, which was organized last year by the young ladies of the college.

During Commencement Week, the society is addressed in the town hall by some prominent man of the State. These exercises are always well attended by the people from town. They are regarded as one of the literary feasts of that week, and excepting the Commencement hop, are probably the most enjoyable, giving all due honor, of course, to the Senior orations; but they are characterized by an incomprehensibleness born of the confused ideas of a four-years' collection which is wonderful to relate, and still more so to hear.

Our meetings are characterized by impromptu speeches, declamations, essays, biographical sketches and debates. Demosthenes might have shaken Greece with his fiery eloquence, Cicero might have caused Rome to tremble with his student-famed (if you will pardon a new term) orations; but some of the men who are being developed by these exercises, will doubtless make a larger area of land than either Greece or Rome had the honor of possessing, to rock as with an earthquake. Many of them will, no doubt, waste their eloquence on the desert air, but it is hoped that all of them may have the honor of testing the walls of our Senate chambers, or of trying the roofs of our places of worship. The gentleman from Washington has more than once put the middle hall in jeopardy already. But the building is old, and as he has not much longer to stay here, it is to be hoped that it will stand just a few more attacks. The sound logic of the gentlemen from Kentucky, Maryland, New York, and Georgia is destined, at no distant period, to cause the world to stop and listen. While the gentlemen from California and Illinois may be classed with the gentleman from Washington, from lack of any intermediate division in our category. But lest we enter too deeply into the realms of prophesy, which is fortunately reserved for the touch of a lighter and more experienced hand, we will cease this strain, and once more return to our historical sphere. You will pardon me for stating here, that, should the editor wish any more histories written to fill the spacious columns of his Alpha, if he will kindly address a communication to, or honor us with a personal call, at No. 8 East Broadway, his wishes will receive the most considerate attention. We solicit correspondence; all orders promptly filled. Now, again for the facts on which Mercury, looking down from his aerial abode, smiles with approving mien.

At present, our society numbers seventeen active, and fourteen honorary members, and is in the best condition that it has experienced since its foundation. All of our members are workers, having the welfare of the society at heart, and recognizing the great benefits to be derived from its exercises. We can only wish it one continued round of success, pledging ourselves to uphold the interests so dear to us, and which are so productive of good results. May it be an organization which will be a benefit to our college, an honor to its founders, and an indispensible aid to the students! May its future members look back on its history with an air of pride, and say: "Vive la Philomathean Societie!"

PIERIA SOCIETY

Motto: Esse Quam Videre.

FOUNDED 1894.

OFFICERS.

PRESIDENT.
MAY L. MATTHEWS.

VICE-PRESIDENT.
CLARA DOWNEY.

SECRETARY.
M. BELLE BOSTON.

TREASURER.
LUCY E. MURRAY.

MEMBERS.

ACTIVE.

Sara E. Beck,
M. Belle Boston,
Clara Downey,
Rose Frazier,
M. Ellen Longfellow,
May L. Matthews,

Lucy E. Murray,
Mary I. Rogers,
Amy C. Russell,
Hallie Toulson,
Marie Westcott,
Grace Whaland.

HONORARY.

Miss Bertha M. Stiles,
Miss Caroline Pettigrew,
Mrs. C. W. Reid,
Mrs. J. R. Micou,

Miss C. S. Wickes,
Miss Mary M. Reiche,
Miss Carrie Anderson,
Miss M. W. Cavender.

SKETCH.

On the tenth of April, 1894, the girls of W. C. met to organize a literary society. Its object was to produce thought among the members, and to give them an education in a pleasant way, in a line that is not included in the regular college course. Miss Stiles, the teacher of French and German at that time, to whom we are indebted for founding this society, was elected chairman pro tem. The first thing accomplished was the selection of a name and motto. The name selected was "Pieria," from Alexander Pope's poem.

> "A little learning is a dangerous thing,
> Drink deep, or taste not the Pierian spring;
> There shallow draughts intoxicate the brain,
> But drinking deeply sobers us again."

The motto adopted was, "Esse quam videre." After the name and motto were chosen and approved, the officers of the first term were elected as follows: Miss Stiles, president; May Matthews, vice-president; Mary W. Cavender, secretary; Grace Whaland, treasurer.

Our meetings are held semi-monthly, and a program is arranged by the president, and is obliged to be carried out by those included, under penalty of a fine (unless some excellent excuse is offered) and the general ill-will of the members, who regard such things as shirking your duty.

PROGRAM.

ORIGINAL ESSAYS.
DECLAMATION
DEBATE.
READING OF THE "PIERIAN."
BIOGRAPHICAL SKETCH.

At first, we tried to include some music in our program, but it so "soothed the savage breasts," and proved such an attraction to the young gentlemen, whose presence was very objectionable, that it was entirely abandoned.

The last Friday in September, and the first Friday after the Xmas holidays, an election of officers takes place. A fee of ten cents is paid by each member for each term. Absence from the regular meetings without good excuse, is considered unpardonable, and a penalty imposed.

A short time before Commencement, the Pierians entertain the other societies of the college. Last year our first reception was given. It was a "five-o'clock tea," and was the success of the season. Our society is yet very young, and not so strong as we would like, but we hope that, as we increase in years, we may accordingly increase in strength.   TREASURER.

Our President.

There isn't a trace of a hoary lock,
    For no ancient dame is she,
But just a gay and merry girl,—
    A student of W. C.

We, the girls of her domain,
    Love her with love supreme,
And pleasing her, we try, " To be
    Rather than to seem "

When we reach our standard height,
    (We are gaining every day)
Then will we all our thanks unite,
    And the honor give to May.

She has labored long and hard
    To make us what we are,
And if we heed the advice she gives,
    We shall be better by far.

Then " three times three " for our President,
    A maiden fair is she,
On getting knowledge she is bent,
    A scholar will she be.

Young Men's Christian Association.

OFFICERS.

PRESIDENT.
R. MERRIKEN.

VICE-PRESIDENT.
G. E. WILLIAMSON.

RECORDING SECRETARY.
E. R. McDORMAN.

CORRESPONDING SECRETARY.
R. L. GLOVER.

TREASURER.
J. A. RICHARDS.

ORGANIST.
J. A. F. CAREY.

Y. M. C. A.

Here again, in the highest aims that should actuate true manhood, Washington stands with her sister colleges, and in her Y. M. C. A. provides for the spiritual development of her students as well as their mental.

An account of that wonderful organization that was begun so humbly fifty-one years ago, in London, by a warehouse clerk, now a baronet of England, need not be given here. Its name is almost a household word throughout the land, and its powerful influence is felt in nearly, if not every city in the world. Indeed, it has been accredited with exerting more influence for good within the church of God than any other organization, excepting perhaps, the Society of Jesus.

But the college Y. M. C. A. is not so widely known. This branch partakes fully of the nature of the great central organization, but is conducted by college students alone, thus enabling it to work in its special sphere better than a mixed association. It was organized about 1877, and in the few years which have elapsed a great change is shown in the spiritual atmosphere of the colleges. Within the last five years, young men have been sent throughout the world, even to far India, China and Japan, bearing greetings from American students to their fellows, and as young men going to young men, they have done a work that no others could. It is of this mighty factor for good that the little band of Washington College students forms a part. The association of the college was organized in 1889, at a meeting of the students called together for the formation of a religious organization. Thus the association is young, and surrounding circumstances indicate an extensive growth.

The association meets in the college chapel on Sunday afternoons, for the usual religious services. At these meetings, an address is delivered by an invited speaker, or in the absence of such, by one of the students capable of performing the duty. At the close of the college year, as part of the exercises, a visiting minister, chosen alternatively from each of the Protestant denominations of the town, delivers in his respective church a sermon before the association. This was delived last year in Emmanuel P. E. Church by Rev. Peregrine Wroth, rector of the Church of the Messiah, Baltimore.

Last summer, our association was one of the two college associations of the State, that sent a delegate to the World's Students Conference at Northfield, Mass.

May God's blessing rest upon these members in their work, and may they have a realization of its import; not only to themselves, but to those about them; those who are now, as they emerge into manhood, forming that character which, for better or worse, will make them a lasting honor or disgrace to their Alma Mater and their country,—a source of pride or shame to many dear ones' hopes.

GLEE CLUB.

OFFICERS.

PRESIDENT.
W. E. B. FAITHFUL.

SECRETARY.
R. L. GLOVER.

BUSINESS MANAGER.
W. E. S. THOMAS.

MEMBERS.

LEADER.
J. A. F. CAREY.

ACCOMPANIST.
C. W. EASLEY.

FIRST TENORS:
C. D. BOSTON.
H. G. SIMPERS.

FIRST BASSOS:
E. R. McDORMAN.
L. A. DAVIS.

SECOND TENORS:
W. E. JACKSON.
E. F. WEBB.

SECOND BASSOS:
H. V. HOLLOWAY.
H. RICKEY.

WARBLER.
HOWARD A. JUMP.

ATHLETIC ASSOCIATION.

OFFICERS.

PRESIDENT,
H. V. HOLLOWAY.

VICE-PRESIDENT,
R. MERRIKEN.

SECRETARY,
T. G. BAXTER.

TREASURER,
A. H. COVEY.

Prof. A. B. Burris, *Director of Gymnasium.*

Athletics.

Prior to 1887 the writer knows very little of the athletic history of Washington College. There are names, however, still on the tongues of former graduates; names of many a famous athlete, flourishing long before the year mentioned, and whose reputations will live right alongside that of the most idolized champion of to-day, and whose deeds of valor on the campus of old Washington will live as long as their admirers have breath to tell the story. In days gone by, in the memory of the Perkins', Pearces', Smiths', Uries', Vickers', Barrolls', and many others that might be mentioned, there could be many a tale told of the prowess of a Hopkins, a Catlin, a Mace, a Todd—men whose glory is still sung at many a gathering, even of the modern athletic crank. In all the years preceding the last seven, the magic diamond was the main sport of the Washington College student. Base-ball occupied his entire attention, and the games were played almost entirely with local organizations. Such a thing as an inter-collegiate contest was unknown, except now and then a game with the ever-hostile foe across the bay—St. John's College. In these contests, so far as the writer knows, the Eastern Shore boys were not always compelled to bite the dust, but more than once came off with flying colors. In those days every village in the county had its ball team; in many cases these clubs were composed of good material, and the contests between college and county were often close and exciting. Chestertown, too, was a foe of the college, and when the writer became connected with the college, the town had held the upper-hand in base-ball for quite a number of years. From that year, however, the college has been growing steadily in athletic strength, until to-day every educational institution in Maryland and Delaware knows of the prowess of Washington College on the ball field, and the inter-collegiate and other contests on the old campus, are the delight of town and county. The local ball organizations are an unknown quantity. No more local contests, except now and then one with the second team. An organization recognized by such institutions as the University of Pennsylvania, is too fast company for the local nine, and the sport-loving community demands better exhibitions.

It might be interesting to note more closely, the growth of base-ball at the college. During the past seven years there have been in attendance among the students, those who possessed some talent in the pitching department. A good pitcher is the mainstay of the whole nine, and good work in the box is bound to insure interest, and most always success. During the period just mentioned three names appear conspicuously in the line mentioned: Stevens, Prettyman and Burris. The first was a terror to neighboring teams, and generally managed to puzzle the very best batsmen. His best work was done, however, against a Baltimore team, the "Browns." He was fortunate enough in that game to have as catcher a young man by the name of Foster, who was visiting Chestertown at the time. The city chaps could do nothing with the doughty pitcher's delivery, and he accomplished the really creditable feat of striking out the side in one inning on nine pitched balls. He won the game by the score of 6 to 8, and his memory is still green in the annals of base-ball at his Alma Mater.

Prettyman, while not having an opportunity to test his strength against any college team, was quite as successful with county clubs, and during his stay was seldom defeated. Porter was the mainstay behind the bat for these two pitchers, while Duer, C. Perkins, Bounds, Beck, Polk, Brice, Clarke and others figured conspicuously in the field. The growing success of the team begat a growing interest in the whole body of students, as well as the citizens of the town. When Prettyman left school, there was no one to take his place. Something must be done to keep up the reputation of the college. Over in Delaware, at the State fair, some of the students had seen a young man by the name of Burris take part in the base-ball exhibitions. Pleased by the strength he showed in the pitcher's box, they were determined, if possible, to induce him to attend college. Ascertaining that his financial condition would not allow his entrance, and finding him willing and anxious to come, not only for the purpose of playing ball, but also for mental improvement, the students and Board of Visitors gave him his expenses, and he was entered as a regular student. His advent marks the beginning of a base-ball career for Washington College, that has ended in placing her at the summit of the mountain of success, and to-day her club poses as the champion college organization of Maryland and Delaware. Burris has landed the team there, but has been most materially aided by such men as Zearfoss, Brice, Woodruff, Blackiston, Polk, Cameron, Armstrong, Massey, Beck, Clymer, Beaston, Franklin, Perkins, Bounds, Boston, Stidham, Deakyne, Davis, Holloway, Faithful, Patton, Brown, and others.

The appearance of Burris on the scene gave an impetus to athletics in another direction. The college had long been in need of a gymnasium. A ghost of one had always existed in the basement of West Hall, but the destructive bump of the genus boy, always largely developed, had reduced it to more than skin and bones, and it had long since been deserted. Through the liberality of the citizens of Chestertown, and the indomitable energy of President Reid, $1200 were raised to put up a building, which was stocked with the necessary apparatus by the Board of Visitors and Governors. These same gentlemen recognizing in Burris a young man "to tie to," sent him to a summer physical training school, and placed him in charge of the gymnasium as physical instructor. The dose of summer training has been repeated, so that to-day the college is far above the average in its gymnastic appointments, and the work done in the gymnasium is on a par with that done by its instructor on the diamond. The results of his training are shown every year by the exhibition given during Commencement week, on what is known as Field Day. This day, too, is an innovation. It is an occasion, so far as Washington College is concerned, only about five years old. Students unskilled in base-ball, have a chance to show what they can do in racing, hurdling, jumping, vaulting, and weight-throwing. These are days of great interest to the town and county. The scene is an animated one. The beautiful terraces of the college are one mass of beautiful feminine faces, relieved by the more sombre forms of admiring men-folk. The contestants in the arena below, strain every nerve in friendly bouts, and some of the work is really fine. The college has not succeeded in breaking many records, probably the best work being done by Brice, whose general athletic work carried off most of the prizes. Parker's work in pole-vaulting is worthy of mention. $9\frac{1}{2}$ feet is seldom beaten by colleges of W. C.'s size, and his beautiful leaps will long be remembered. Every year improves the exhibitions of Field Day, and the time is not far distant when the records of old Washington in track events, will stand with credit alongside those of other colleges.

Foot-ball has run about the same course in the past seven years as base-ball, tho' not with the same success. The first inter-collegiate foot-ball battle, and probably the first foot-ball contest ever played on the campus, was fought with old St. John's. Reader, probably you will remember that. St. John's was then in the flower of her strength. That year she won the championship of the South. Washington College hardly knew what a foot-ball was. There could be no other outcome. The game resulted, St. John's 119, W. C. 0. That knocked all the foot-ball out of the defeated team for awhile. But such spirits as Porter, Twilley, Usilton, Brice (the two last known as the Siamese twins, on account of their inseparable runs across the field together), Polk, Merriken, Knotts, Perkins, Butler, Massey, Duer and others, would not let the invigorating sport die; and through the efforts of these men, with such later-day additions as Zearfoss, Davis, Holloway, Patton, Harris, Blackiston and others, have managed to hold up the honor of the college on the foot-ball field. The sport is not as popular as base-ball, however, and consequently, there is not so much interest; the danger attending its play detracting from its enjoyment. Still, W. C. has tackled nearly all the colleges of the State, and, while never being able to defeat its old rival, St. John's, still the score has been greatly reduced since the 119-to-0 game.

In lighter athletics, such as tennis and croquet, the less muscular students have freely indulged. The fine grounds of the college afford excellent turf for these sports, and they are freely indulged in. The older alumnus must look back and wonder over the advance of the college in athletics, and, indeed, along every line. In these days of bicycling and bloomers, and lady students, old W. C. has a chance to be the proud possessor of the coming woman; and, if predictions come true, she will take, in her course through life, the place of the man on the athletic field. Reader, think of it.

In conclusion, W. C. has reason to be proud of her vast improvement in muscle as well as brain. The college spirit seems to have grown, and the student is proud of his Alma Mater, and willing to work for her. Let such spirit spread, and our Eastern Shore venerable institution will hold its head up among the proudest of the land.

Athletic Association Contests,

JUNE 19, 1894.

EVENT.	WINNER.	RECORDS.	PRIZES.
HURDLE RACE, (110 yds.)	E. B. POLK	17½ seconds	SILVER CUP.
RUNNING HIGH JUMP	E. B. POLK	4 FEET 8 INCHES	GOLD CUFF BUTTONS.
100-YARD DASH	T. MASSEY	11 seconds	GOLD MEDAL.
100 YARDS, (under 16 years.)	R. SIMPERS	13 seconds	GOLD MEDAL.
THROWING BASE-BALL	D. C. BEASTON	101 yards	GOLD CUFF BUTTONS.
RUNNING LONG JUMP	{ E. B. POLK { T. MASSEY	17 FEET 6 INCHES 17 FEET 5 INCHES	GOLD CHARM.
POTATO RACE	B. H. DASHIELL		CUFF BUTTONS.
MILE RUN	E. B. POLK	6 MINUTES	GOLD PEN.

FOOT-BALL.

SEASON OF '94.

MANAGER,
A. B. BURRIS.

CAPTAIN,
R. MERRIKEN.

RUSHERS,

H. V. HOLLOWAY,
M. PATTON,
L. A. DAVIS,
S. T. COOPER,
R. MERRIKEN,
S. R. DOUGLAS,
D. W. T. ZEARFOSS,

QUARTER-BACK,

T. MASSEY.

HALF-BACKS,

C. D. BOSTON, R. L. GLOVER.

FULL-BACK,

A. B. BURRIS.

SUBSTITUTES.

T. G. BAXTER, W. C. BROWN,
H. F. PERKINS. R. J. NICHOLSON.

RECORD OF GAMES:

WASHINGTON COLLEGE vs. STILL POND A. C.. . . 22—0
WASHINGTON COLLEGE vs. ST. JOHN'S COLLEGE, 8—24
WASHINGTON COLLEGE vs. STILL POND A. C., . . 0—0
WASHINGTON COLLEGE vs. MD. AGRICULTURAL COLLEGE, 0—12
WASHINGTON COLLEGE vs. STILL POND A. C.. . . 18—0
WASHINGTON COLLEGE vs. JOHNS HOPKINS, . 12—0

Boston, Glover, Douglas, Cooper,
Zearfoss, Harris, Brice, Brown,
Davis, Merrick, Massey, Holloway, Patton.

FOOT BALL TEAM '94.

BASE-BALL

SEASON OF '94.

A. B. BURRIS, P. AND CAPTAIN.

GEORGE BRICE, 1B.,   W. C. BLACKISTON, L. F.,
E. B. POLK, 3B.,   H. V. HOLLOWAY, C. F.,
J. M. ARMSTRONG, S. S.,   C. D. BOSTON, R. F.,
A. V. WOODRUFF, 2B.,   D. W. T. ZEARFOSS, C.

SUBSTITUTES:

D. C. BEASTON,   T. MASSEY.

N. CAMERON.

MANAGER.   UMPIRE.
H. N. PERKINS.   PROF. E. J. CLARKE.

RECORD—SEASON OF '94.

WASHINGTON VS. BALTIMORE CITY COLLEGE,	21—4
WASHINGTON VS. NEW WINDSOR COLLEGE,	4—1
WASHINGTON VS. DEICHMANN SCHOOL,	8—2
WASHINGTON VS. ST. JOHN'S COLLEGE,	4—5
WASHINGTON VS. BALTIMORE CITY COLLEGE,	6—3
WASHINGTON VS. BALTIMORE Y. M. C. A.,	8—0
WASHINGTON VS. MONUMENTALS, BALTIMORE,	8—9
WASHINGTON VS. JOHNS HOPKINS UNIVERSITY,	9—2
WASHINGTON VS. LUTHERVILLE O. C.,	4—5
WASHINGTON VS. FEDERALSBURG A. C.,	5—0

BASE-BALL

SEASON OF '95.

D. W. T. ZEARFOSS, C. AND CAPTAIN.

B. F. DEAKYNE, 2B.,	A. B. BURRIS, P.,
N. CAMERON, S. S.,	L. A. DAVIS, 1B.,
C. D. BOSTON, L. F.,	C. S. BROWN, C. F.,
J. G. C. STIDHAM, 3B.,	T. MASSEY, R. F.

SUBSTITUTES:

H. V. HOLLOWAY.   W. E. B. FAITHFUL.

M. PATTON.

GAMES PLAYED:

APRIL 17.	WASHINGTON vs. JOHNS HOPKINS,		7—6
" 20.	WASHINGTON vs. BALTIMORE CITY,		12—9
MAY 1.	WASHINGTON vs. MT. ST. MARY'S,	(postponed)	
" 4.	WASHINGTON vs. PEABODY,		9—3
" 11.	WASHINGTON vs. MD. AGRICULTURAL, (unfinished)		3—4
" 15.	WASHINGTON vs. CLINTON A. C.,		8—12
" 18.	WASHINGTON vs. JOHNS HOPKINS,	(postponed)	

GAMES TO BE PLAYED:

MAY 25. WASHINGTON vs. W. M. C.,

JUNE 1. WASHINGTON vs. NEW WINDSOR,

" 3. WASHINGTON vs. PENNSYLVANIA UNIVERSITY,

" 8. WASHINGTON vs. CLINTON A. C.,

" 12. WASHINGTON vs. MT. ST. JOSEPH'S,

COMMENCEMENT DAY. WASHINGTON vs. MONUMENTALS.

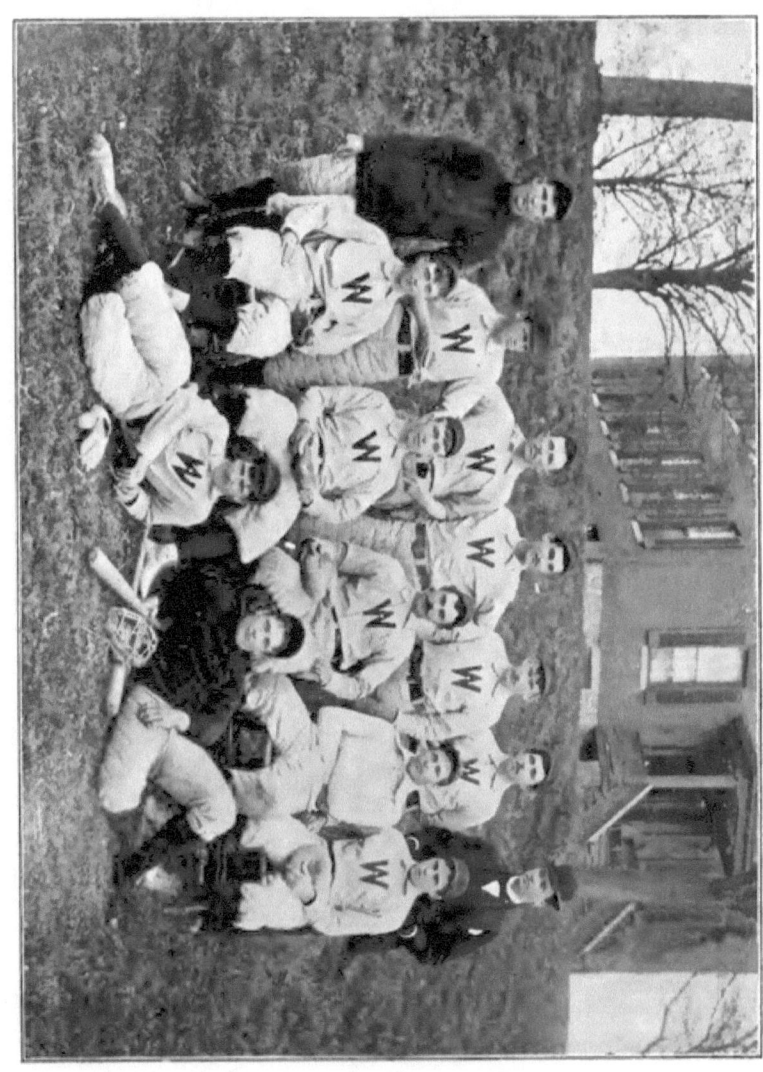

Brown, Harris, Davis, Holloway, Faithful, Boston, Perkins,
Deakyne, Stidham, Zearfoss, Brice, Massey (Manager),
Cawerou, Fulton.

BASE BALL TEAM '95.

Alumni Association.

FIRST PRESIDENT,

HON. E. F. CHAMBERS, LL. D.

PRESIDENT,

COLIN F. STAM, A. M.

VICE-PRESIDENTS,

W. FRANK HINES, M. D.,

JAS. E. ELLEGOOD.

JOHN D. URIE, Esq.

RECORDING SECRETARY,

FRED. G. USILTON.

CORRESPONDING SECRETARY,

PROF. J. S. W. JONES, A. M.

TREASURER,

H. L. DODD, M. D.

The annual meeting of the Association is held on Tuesday of Commencement Week, at 3 P. M. The Alumni Banquet is held at Shuster's Dining Parlors, followed by addresses by some members.

Our Alumni.

Not many years ago, within the memory of the writer, a few of the energetic graduates of our esteemed Alma Mater organized themselves into an Alumni Association. It was a stride indicative of progress, for it serves to impress upon one the fact, that our connection with, and interest in the college of our choice should not cease with our exit from its halls. Indeed, we should realize that a new duty confronts us as soon as we launch our barks upon the stormy sea of life; for it is not so much the student's duty to maintain the honor and integrity of the institution, as it is the obligation of those to whom the outside world looks for the best evidences of the true worth and advantages of the college whence the alumnus comes. The world to-day really knows little of what is actually going on within our college halls, save the routine of recitation and lecture. It has no opportunity to judge of the merits of the college curriculum, for the simple reason that student life is an existence apart from the world—it is merely the vantage ground in the great complement of life's activities. Catalogues may picture the advantages of the institution in the most glowing terms, and may make the whole thing a veritable fountain whence flows naught save knowledge pure; but as the tree is known by its fruit, so is the standard of the college to be determined by the ability and worth of its graduates. Not many colleges of the State of Maryland, of the same rank as Washington College, can boast of so bright an array of alumni as she. In every vocation in life, she has sons who are an honor to her, an honor to themselves, and a power in the world for good. In the halls of State, whether it be in that office which is the highest gift of the people of a State, or whether it is in legislative or judicial assemblies, her alumni are among the foremost in the ranks. The present governor of the State of Delaware was once a student at the timehonored institution ; Maryland's honored and popular comptroller was also a student here. The name of the junior U. S. Senator from Maryland is also to be found among the alumni of our college, and the late Hon. George Vickers, whose name is honored by all who knew him, and whose labors in the halls of the U. S. Senate resulted in so much good to his State, laid the foundation for that vast fund of knowledge which he possessed in the class-rooms of Washington College. The late Hon. R. F. Brattan, who figured so prominently in our national legislature, was also a graduate of this institution. Such a hasty survey of our college's worthy sons is sufficient, I think, to prove that the present generation of alumni need not be ashamed of the material she has "turned out." I think I am not far short of the truth, when I say that there is not one of her graduates, either in years past, or in recent years, but that holds some position of honor and responsibily in life. Washington College has manifested through her alumni, that she is worthy of the patronage and support of the people of the territory from which she draws her students, and, indeed, more. But then, there remains something more to be done. This little Alumni Association, which was started years ago, is a progressive organization ; indeed, it has made wonderful strides. It has created an interest in the college which did not exist before its organization ; it has brought the graduates of the past face to face with those of the present, and has made each of us feel that our interest in our Alma Mater should be active rather than passive. The relation of an alumnus to a college, is similiar in many respects to that of an agent to the company which he represents. We must use our influence upon the young men who are seeking an education higher than that attainable in the common schools, to bring them into our college; and there are graduates enough of Washington College scattered throughout the land, who, by setting forth the advantages of the institution, could swell the number on her roll to double the present attendance. We must labor for the good of the association of which we are members. Endeavor to impress upon those who are not now members, the importance of enlisiting in the ranks; and we must not lose sight of the fact, that our Alma Mater's claim is a just one, worthy of our attention, worthy of our esteem, and still more worthy of our efforts for her good. Let us all endeavor to raise high the standard of our dear old institution; let us publish abroad her merits, and may we ever be an honor and an ornament to that institution of which, I trust, we are proud to be alumni. A MEMBER OF '90.

College Reminiscences.

In his very carefully prepared article on Washington College, which appeared in a recent "History of Education in Maryland," Professor Rowland Watts thus writes, referring to the early administration of Professor William J. Rivers: "The college became noted for the high moral character of its young men, as it formerly was for their disorderly and immoral conduct." It was the distinctive privilege of the "Immortal Seven," as we of the class of '76 modestly styled ourselves, to share in the malodorous reputation of the old regime, as well as to bask in the glory of being the first graduates (that is, the first he cared to claim) under Professor Rivers; and no class could more fittingly have served as a connecting link, for among our number were certain prodigal spirits who, demoralized by former evil associations, still wandered in a far country, as well as those who proved themselves in every way worthy to receive the broader culture and finer manners introduced by Professor Rivers. A single instance of each will suffice: One of our number, in company with, and led by a member of an advanced class, denied himself the pleasure (for he had been carefully brought up) of going to church one fine Sunday morning, and spent the time in making a key to fit the lock of a store-room, in which were several barrels of apples belonging to a professor who lodged with us in the west building. During the weeks that followed, the apples, so long as they lasted, served as bribes to other students to do the work that should have been done by these degenerate seekers after knowledge, and poor old Fred, our colored factotum, who was honesty itself, rested under a cloud. In one of the incursions to the room, among the plunder found was a bottle, the contents of which so nearly resembled the rare old

Falernian raved over by Horace, that it was determined to remove the temptation from the pathway of our misguided professor. This was accomplished so successfully, that the man representing the higher class (we have always felt a pardonable pride in knowing that it was not our member) was found not long after on the campus, to use one of Bret Harte's expressive phrases, "in a frightfully dissolute state."

On the other hand, in our Smith we had one of the most studious men who ever went through a college. He employed much of his leisure time in reading Latin and Greek books not in the curriculum, while the most of us found no end of difficulty in reading those that were. And just here, a lesson which may be helpful: One day, before an important examination in Greek, for which some of us had been most diligently preparing for the last few days, Smith was asked, "Why are you so indifferent; why are you not preparing?" His reply was characteristic and to the point,—"I knew this was coming; I have been preparing for it all along; I am now ready to meet it." It is scarcely necessary to say that he was always primus inter pares, and easily took the first honors of the class.

It was the proud distinction of a member of our class to be the first man lost in Chestertown, and his adventure had quite a historic sequence. Being completely enraptured by the charms of one of the young ladies of the town (and who of us has not been?), with whom he had been most diligently studying astronomy on the bridge (and, oh, that bridge! what an institution it was in those days! Some of us had far more real pleasure there than ever Napoleon felt at Lodi, although it never made us quite so famous), he became hopelessly tangled up in streets in his efforts to return to college, and had to inquire the way of a belated citizen. When the good people learned that the place was large enough for one to become lost in (they didn't know the true inwardness of the story), they became so elated that then and there began those improvements which have, it is said, made the sleepy old village one of the most wide-awake and progressive towns of Eastern Maryland.

To produce its most beautiful women,—such as Helen of Troy, Hypatia of Alexandria, and fair Rosamond of England—nature has required different climes and far-removed centuries; but sometimes she is prodigal of even her best things, and in 1873-76 she gave to Chestertown a wealth of youth and beauty, "daughters of the gods, divinely tall, and most divinely fair," that made it the centre of the social refinement and culture of the Eastern Shore. Many of these were as good as beautiful, and to-day the men of '76 have only grateful thanks to render for their helpful and uplifting influence.

A Member of '76.

Recent Graduates.

It is especially interesting to see what the alumni have been doing in the educational line—in teaching and in building higher the superstructure whose foundations have been laid at Washington College. The teaching fraternity embraces within its ranks some of our brightest men, and it is not to be overlooked that the Alumni furnishes to Alma Mater her professor of mathematics and astronomy. Professors in other institutions, several county superintendents in various States, and our representation in the graduate departments of the Universities is very naturally a matter of pride.

B. F. Perkins, '92, has for two years pursued a regular law course at the University of Pennsylvania, and has shown such great talent that he has been unanimously elected class orator.

H. N. Perkins, '94, has been pursuing his studies at Drexel Institute, Philadelphia.

At Johns Hopkins, Washington College is represented by J. W. Chapman, Jr., '92, and A. M. Hanna, '93.

I. L. Twilley, A. M., has finished a course in science at the University of Nebraska, and received the Ph. D. degree.

At Drew Theological Seminary, E. A. Robinson, '93, has pursued his studies with great distinction, and secured the degree of B. D.

B. F. Parker and R. C. Leaverton are pursuing their studies in the Department of Civil Engineering, at Cornell University.

The position these Alumni are making for themselves, and for this college, is an enviable one. Among the last year's graduates, U. L. Gordy is principal of Sharptown High School, and C. C. Brown is holding a similar position, while E. B. Polk is first assistant postmaster at Princess Anne.

EDITORIALS.

HEIKEL, heikel, heikel, siss-boom-ah !
Rick-a-rack-a, Washington, rah, rah, rah !

TWELVE Seniors for '95.

WE TAKE pleasure here in expressing our thanks in behalf of the Junior class, to the Trustees and Faculty, who have aided us greatly in the publication of this volume.

UNIFORMLY, we have met with the kindest encouragement. To all who have helped us in suggestion, or in more substantial ways, we extend our thanks, only regretting that space limits forbid mentioning names.

THE classification of students in this volume is the same as that of the catalogue. We expect more or less fault to be found with this plan, but no better one suggested itself to us.

THE class leadership prizes given by members of the Board of Trustees, is another indication of the W. C. boom. Ere long, we hope to see similar prizes offered in a department where they will probably redound as much honor to the college as the present ones. We refer to the department of composition. Our students must educate themselves in this work, and they need encouragement.

THIS ANNUAL has been prepared very hurriedly. All the general composition has been done in the last few weeks; individual work prevented the editors from beginning this book as early in the year as they would have liked. We hope our readers will indulgently overlook a number of rather serious typographical errors.

WE ARE pleased to announce, that the "Manual of Zoology," which has been carefully and ably prepared by Prof. Stephens, assisted by Messrs. Brown and Davis, is in the binder's hands, and will soon be ready for use in the class-room. The compilation of a text-book is a stride indicative of great progress at Washington College, and it will certainly meet with great success.

IN REGARD to the over-sensitiveness to jesting and cartooning manifested by many of our patrons, our philosophy is about this: That the sooner one is educated out of such a spirit by a succession of sturdy, independent annuals, the better it will be for himself and everybody concerned; that feeling hurt where some personal crankiness is ridiculed, is confessing that the man, with all his perfections, is not able to renounce this one silly shortcoming; and that the wise man will join with his jesters, and, by laughing at his follies, rise above them. We should remember the difficulty of holding the mind itself down to our ideal of what we ought to be; and that, by the time the idea reverberates in the perverse members of the body, innumerable chances of absurdity have offered. Few of us can hope even in time, to educate ourselves wholly out of the dominion of the ludicrous. If, then, you have been cartooned, bear it like a man. Show by your actions, that you have outgrown that folly; for the editors have tried to prevent anything from entering this volume through a spirit of maliciousness, and hence have no apologies to offer. YE EDITOR.

SENIOR REFLECTIONS.

A SENIOR.

BROWN: I would rather dwell at Boston'(s) than with Princess Anne.

CAMERON: I er-would like to er-a-return if they could teach me baseball.

CAREY: The world may be hard, but no worse than those Pig Alleyites when I want to study.

COPPER: Many, great, and most useful are the results of my college days. I have learned to raise a mustache, and I've—forgot what else.

HOLLOWAY: I would reluctantly yet willingly sever the many fond ties of friendships which bind me to my Alma Mater, if the brightness of Summer would last all the year.

MISS MATTHEWS: May will last.

MERRIKEN: I would willingly go if I were sure of my Christmas Car(r)ol(l).

NICHOLSON: I go willingly. I have no more to cipher.

SIMPERS: How can we leave the girls?

PERKINS: Let's don't, let's take one apiece with us.

Senior Haps.

Dr. Reid: "Who did the most of the work in Virginia in early days?"

Merriken: "Jail birds."

Easley: "Who was Proser pina?"

Nicholson (Senior): "Wife of Plato."

Prof. in Physics: "Mr. Perkins, of what value are Geissler's tubes to scientists?"

Mr. Perkins: "They look pretty when the electricity gets to wandering around in them."

A Junioress: "Mr. H., come up next period, 'Mumps' wants you."

Can anybody tell us where "Daddy" C.'s "fluke" is? We didn't suppose anyone knew, and strange to say, neither does he.

Mr. B., (taking a stroll with Miss ——): "Isn't that a queer looking pig over there in that vacant lot, Miss E—?"

Miss E., (coolly, as animal in question raises its head): "It is indeed. In fact, it is the first one I ever saw with horns and a goat—ee!"

What are the eighty-four rules of the heart? All the Seniors know of course, but for the benefit of those who don't, we would refer you to Allen & Greenoughs' Grammar, page 381.

Miss P.: "Mr. V., from your conversation one would be led to suppose that you are not very fond of ladies' company."

"Doc" V.: "I'm not."

Miss P.: "Then please excuse me." (Exit.)

First Senior: "Why is it that R. is so fond of whistling 'Listen to the Mocking Bird,' in the spring?"

SECOND SENIOR: "Because then his feathered friends are fresh from the South, and remind him of the Palmcr)etto State, of course."

FIRST SENIOR (crushed): "Oh!"

"What is Mr. P.'s favorite wild-flower?"

Of the exact botanical name we are ignorant, but it belongs to the family "Rosacea."

FIRST MAIDEN: "Why are lace curtains so repulsive to Mr. S.?"

SECOND MAIDEN: "I suppose it's because through them one sometimes gets a peep behind the scenes."

MR. C.: "Billy, run across and tell Miss E. that I would like to walk down town with her."

LITTLE WILLIE (running toward Miss E., who is walking rapidly toward town): "Na, wait a minute." Miss E., (after having received the above communication)—"Oh, pshaw!"

MISS MATTHEWS' ONLY PRAYER: "I am the first girl graduate; O! please write a nice poem on me."

INSTRUCTOR IN ETHICS: "Mr. C., if you have done wrong, what is the first thing you should do on reconsidering the action?"

Still small voice of a Junior from over the way: "Thrust it from you."

MR. C. (aloud): "Trust on God."

INSTRUCTOR: "How? He is usually a good one to trust in, but He doesn't apply here. Next."

PROF. MICOU (to class '95): "I don't know which I dread more, commencement day or Judgment day."

The Shaved Pig.

A long-nosed rooter on our campus trespassed,
    Looking for something to eat;
A few of our high-toned students went past,
    And enticed Mr. Pig to a feast.

The owner of the quadruped next came along,
    Full of revenge on the boys;
The whereabouts of the animal couldn't be found,
    Because he stirred not up a noise.

Then up to "Pig Alley" his pigship was taken,
    And down on the table he sat;
While razors were whetted and lather was shaken,
    The boys and the pig had a chat.

Come along "Mr. Pig" and receive your just dues.
    We'll take off part of your dressing;
So off with the hair and his dirty black hues,
    Those razors did give him a blessing.

JUNIOR VITASCOPE.

	Age.	Nick names	Pastime	Favorite Authors	Politics	Color of eyes	Favorite expressions	Disposition	Remarkable for	Favorite resort.	Destiny.
Boston	Sweet sixteen	"Becky."	Longing.	Browning	"Whate'er his is."	Brown.	"Delas knows."	Amative.	Smiles & Conceit.		Mrs. B.
Burchical	x	"Lady."	Thinking.	Allen and Or 'nough	Woman's Suffrage.	Yellow.	"Goodness."	Bashful.	Energy.	Class room	Old Maid.
Douglass	19x	"Pock"	Sleeping	Judge, etc	Free Whiskey	Red	"O, yes."	Foppish.	Brass		Clown.
Early	17x	"Jack."	Having fun.	Can't read.	Republican	Hazel	"By grab!"	Important.	Scholarship		N ihil.
Glover	21x	"Chips."		Stowe	People's Party.	Black.	"By Gimminie."	Slow.	Age.	In Mac's room.	Bachelor.
Jump	20x	"Sis."	Smoking	JesseJames Mag'a sup.		Green.	"Come off."	Ilous.	Voice.	Bed.	Quack.
McDormon	16	"Mac."	Killing Jack.	"Sowl any of 'em."	Prohibition	Gray.	"Don't yr like it?"	Tough.	Forget- fulness	Before the Mirror	Silver- Tongue Orator.
Noble	18x	"Ned."	Going down town.	Duchess	Labor par'y	Pink.	"Molly Moses"	Gay.	Tongue.	Laboratory	Tramp.
Uelton	16x	"Doke."	Walking.	Newspaper.	Democrat.	White.	"Let er go."	Grave.	Vanity.	Table	Politician.

Junior Quotations.

"I would like to go, but I am troubled with heart failure."—EASLEY.

"O, what do I want to go for?"—GLOVER.

"I could go if I wanted to."—McDORMAN.

"I have no time to be social during the college months, but in the summer I am a Belle."—MISS BELLE BOSTON.

"I would rather tease the boys than go with the girls."—DOUGLAS.

"You need not bother about me, I am ———. O!"—MISS BURCHINAL.

"Hang 'em! I would rather loaf."—USILTON.

"I have no time to bother with the girls."—NOBLE.

"I am a lady myself."—JUMP.

SCALDS.

PURCHASER—"How often does your annual come out?"
DOUGLAS——"Twice a week."

LADY (in astronomy class)—"Professor, what effect has the moon upon the tide?"
PROF. JONES—"None, but lots on the untied."

NOBLE (in drug store)—"What's them?"
MAC—"Moth balls."
NOBLE—"What'er they fit for?"

EASLEY—"I called on Miss Murray awhile ago."
DOUGLASS—"Did; did you go in?"
EASLEY—"E—er—no. Sick."
DOUGLASS—"What was the matter?"
EASLEY—"Heart Failure."

"Why is 'Chips' Glover the most sentimental student of '96?"
"Because he is a (G)lover."

"Although this is a (Noble) class it is (Easley) converted to a hop, skip and (Jump) assembly."

"Why will Miss Burchinal keep splendid order in a school-room?"

"Because she will remind her pupils of the birch."

PROF. MICOU—"Mr. McDorman, what is Virgil's greatest work?"

MAC.—"Virgil."

BROWN—"Becky, why are you always saying ''Tis mighty sweet, yet, oh! how bitter, to love a girl and then not git her?' It makes me feel strange."

BELLE (blushing)—"Say that again I have been waiting for that two years."

Virgil Class, Jump reading.—"Varium et mutabile semper femina."

PROF. MICOU—"Better omit that, there is a lady present."

WHAT THEY DON'T DO IN THE LABORATORY.

Scenes in the Science Department.

ANTHONY (in dissecting room).—"Professor what would you do if that scapel was to get dull?"

PROF. STEPHENS—"Sharpen it."

MASSEY (in laboratory).—"Professor, where is the concentrated solution of H_2O?"

PROFESSOR—"In the pump."

PROF. STEPHENS (in Physiology)—Mr. Janvier, what is the color of the red corpuscles of the blood?"

JANVIER—"Green."

PROFESSOR—"No."

JANVIER—"O yes, blue."

Sophomore Kodaks.

BRINSFIELD—"Don't tread on my toes."
COVEY—"Old edition."
COULBOURNE—"He wants an office."
CRUIKSHANK—"Carry me pig-a-back."
FAITHFUL—"Successful hunter (no results)."
FOWLER—"Just superb."
GRAHAM—"Momentary barber."
HURTT—"Lost his heart."
QUILLEN—"Personified homesickness."
THOMAS—"Class dude."
WEBB—"Too sweet for anything."

SCALDS.

DR. REID (at end of month)—"Mr. Webb you have two lessons in Greek to make up."

WEBB—"Doctor, I was sick three days."

DOCTOR—"How? 'Twas a miscount on your part, Mr. Webb, prepare to make them up to-morrow."

BECK—"What is the past tense of 'I shall'?"

THOMAS—"I have shalled."

DR. REID—"What is the plural of he?"

COVEY—"Hees."

OMNES STUDENTES—"O, Brinsfield, how much did you pay for Miss Russell's lunch at shoe box festival?"

BRINSFIELD—"One dollar and five cents."

OMNES STUDENTES—"Gee whiz!"

BRINSFIELD—"Why it was worth $5.00."

O. S.—"Such shoes!!!"

PROFESSOR (at banquet)—"What did they do with the wine?"

GRAHAM—"She washed his feet with it."

That Tin Horn.

When the earth is clad with beauty,
    And the world is full of life,
'Tis a pity that a tin-horn,
    Should be the cause of so much strife.

Can't a fellow show his feeling
    When a victory is won?
Are people made of soberness
    Without a spark of fun?

When a person is young and lively,
    He naturally is naughty,
But maybe when he teaches Greek
    He, too, will become haughty.

And lecture the young gentleman
    Who disturbs the study hours
Of the students striving bravely
    With o'er strained mental powers.

But we take some comfort
    Because our dear team won,
And tooting horns during the game
    Is such a lot of fun.

And though we do get lectured,
    We know our team can win;
We'll blow at game for championship,
    Horns far worse than tin.

Freshman Scalds.

Prof. Micou—"Miss Frazier, what are the principal parts of the verb 'to be sick'?"

Miss F. (thinking of last evening)—"Simpo—ere—psi—simptum."

Davis (in Botany)—"Professor, why, ah-if a person should stick the bud end of a willow twig in the ground leaving the branch out would the roots go upward?"

Professor—"Try it."

A. McCabe—"Is everything that moves and keeps still air?"

Patton (at society banquet)—"Say, boys, what kind of food is that first French word 'menu?'"

Chum (sotto voice)—"I don't know, send out and see."

Patton—"Waiter, bring me a small dish of me-n-you."

"Why are the Misses Stam so near in government employ?"

"Because it only takes one letter to make them a stamp."

E. McCabe—"Is there a house in town with two damsels in it?"

Douglass—"No."

McCabe—"Just my luck; no 'dear' to keep 'mamma' off while I escape to the parlor."

Green Freshy (in millinery store thinking of unpaid wash bill)—"Do you keep celluloid ribbon for college colors."

"Why does Pardee walk with his head on top?"

"Because of the difference of weight between his feet and head."

PATTON (with his girl at soda water fountain)—"It's not often I get to town, but when I do I make the money fly, give me a cent's worth of soda water."

CLERK—"What flavor?"

PATTON—"Soda water."

Wild forms of hazing.

Prep. Scalds.

Prof. M—" Mr. Coursey, what is the stem of culpa?"
Coursey—" Miss Culp."

Prof. Clarke—" What is the singular of swine?"
Miss Wilkins—" Hog."

Admiring Soph (to prep)—Why does not Miss Longfellow wear that charming little red cap instead of that straw?"
Prep.—" Dunno, spec she wants something bigger to put her knowle-g- in."

" Why is Miss Whaland like an eight-day clock?"
" Both run a weak (week)."

Prep—" Mr. Douglass, what will you call the Annual?"
Douglas—" Alpha."
Prep—" Appropriate name, what does it mean?"

> " I never would give a kiss," said Lou,
> " To man, for I abhor it."
> She never would *give* a kiss 'tis true,
> But she'd *take* one and thank you for it.

Professor (severe and dignified)—What was the cause of the Revolutionary War?"
Prep (fearful and trembling)—" They rang the old Liberty Bell, until they cracked it, and had a fight over it."

Miss Rogers (strolling on the bridge)—" Shoo! That bee is after the honey on my flowers."
Vickers (killing it with his hat)—No, there is another bee after that honey."

A Soliloquy.

A flunk or not a flunk—that is the question:
Whether 'tis nobler in the mind to enter
A class-room and take a zip,
Or to pony and make a ten,
And, by ponying pass? To pass,—to flunk,—
No more; and by passing to say we end
The horrid fear and a thousand shames
That flunking would incur—'tis a consummation
Goodly to be wished. To pass,—to flunk,—
To pony! perchance to be caught! ay, there's the rub;
For in that delection, what horrors may come!
That's what makes ponying so apprehensive;
For who would bear the scoffs and jeers of college,
The professor's scorn, the bright students' ridicule,
The pangs of mocking and unsuccessful effort,
The reproach of his class and the spurns
His family would heap upon him
When he himself might safely pass
With a few notes? Who would tax his mind
And grunt and sweat wearily over books,
But that the dread of something following,
Makes us rather think of awful grinding,
Than to leap the gulf with a pony?
Thus fear of "fire" makes cowards of us all;
And thus the mighty power of resolution
Is vanquished by the ghastly thought
Of the Prof's good eye at exam's,
And ventures of great risk and issue,
With this regard expire ignominiously
And lose the name of action.

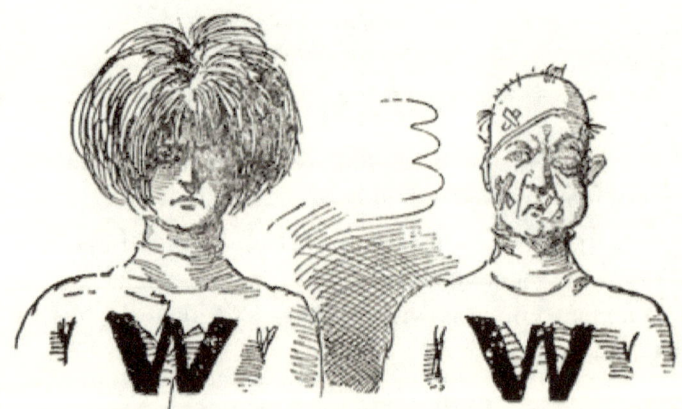

BEFORE AND AFTER THE FOOT-BALL GAME.

Opera Varii Generis.

Mrs. Micou (after Thanksgiving)—"Mr. Micou, one of my best chickens is gone."

Prof. M.—"The boys converted it to a Thanksgiving turkey."

What does Prof. S. enjoy more than ladies' society—"Buckwheat cakes for breakfast."

Why is the Pieria a charitable society?—"Because it has a 'Foster' child."

Lost,—a heart in the room adjoining the laboratory.

"Findin's is keepin's."

Score-keeper (baseball)—"Stidham at the bat, Burris on deck."

"Deak"—"He's not on deck, he is on the terrace talking to those ladies."

"Why should Mr. Melvin watch his 'chickens'?"

"The 'Fowler' will catch her if he don't."

What Others Think of Us.

" Noble by birth, yet nobler by great deeds."—*Longfellow*.

" Ignorance is the curse of God;
  Knowledge, the wings wherewith we fly to Heaven."—*Shakespeare*.

" Night is the Sabbath of mankind,
  To rest the body and the mind."—*Butler*.

" Errors, like straws, upon the surface flow;
  He who would seek pearls must dive below."—*Dryden*.

" To me the meanest flower that blows can give,
  Thoughts that do often lie too deep for tears."—*Wordsworth*.

" Years following years, steal something every day;
  At last they steal us from ourselves away."—*Pope*.

" Self-reverence, self-knowledge, self-control,
  These three alone lead life to sovereign power."—*Tennyson*.

" Index-learning turns no student pale,
  Yet holds the eel of science by the tail."—*Pope*.

X   x   x   x   x   x   x   x   x   —*Our marks*

ADVERTISE YOUR BUSINESS IN

THE CHESTERTOWN TRANSCRIPT,

THE LEADING PAPER OF KENT COUNTY, MD.

JOB AND BOOK WORK

OF ALL KINDS DONE IN THE NEATEST STYLE AT REASONABLE PRICES.

☞ Orders for Engraving and Lithographing promptly filled.

JEFFRES & ROGERS,

Leading Photographers,

Crayon Portraits a Specialty!

SPECIAL ATTENTION GIVEN TO COLLEGE STUDENTS.

JEFFRES & ROGERS,

112 N. Charles Street, - - - Baltimore, Md.

GEORGE BRICE,

—DEALER IN—

Fine Cigars, Tobacco,

FRUITS

AND CONFECTIONERY.

GEO. BRICE,
CHESTERTOWN, MD.

KENT COUNTY'S
LEADING LIVERY,

G. B. McWHORTER.

CHESTERTOWN, MD.

MY TEAMS are First-class in every particular, and satisfaction always given to my customers. Traveling salesmen conveyed to all parts of the Peninsula at moderate prices. Teams for private parties furnished at short notice. Give me a call. Resp'y, etc.,

GEO. B. McWHORTER,
CHESTERTOWN, MD.

Shuster's Dining Parlors

CHESTERTOWN, MD.

Front Street, Opposite the Old Bank.

Permanent and Transient Boarders taken at low rates. Lunch served at short notice. Oysters in all styles. First Class Dinners to country people at 35c. Bride's Cakes made to order. We also carry in stock a general assortment of CAKES and CONFECTIONERY. Picnics and Festivals supplied with our celebrated Ice Cream at moderate prices. A call solicited,

Shuster's Dining Parlors.

FOR FINE PHOTOS, LARGE
PORTRAITS & VIEWS.

—GO TO—

VIRGINIA PHOTO CO.,
Chestertown. Md.

WM. S. CULP.   ALWYN M. CULP.

W. S. & A. M. CULP,

Contractors & Builders,

AND MANUFACTURERS OF

SASH, DOORS, BLINDS,
FRAMES, MOULDINGS,
BRACKETS AND
STAIR WORK.

Plans and Estimates Furnished.

☞ Mill and Office at Railroad Station, Chestertown, Md.

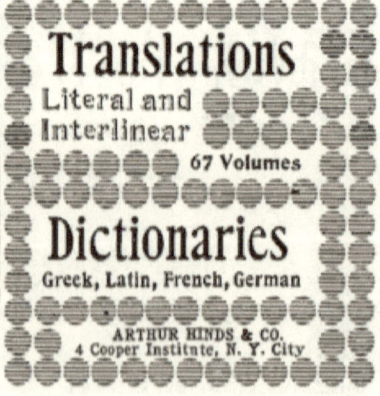

J. H. SIDES,
The Jeweler,

OPPOSITE STAM'S HALL.   CHESTERTOWN, MD.

School Medals and Badges Made to Order.

W. R. MAUL & CO.,
—DEALERS IN—

Confectionery,
FRUITS,
CIGARS, TOBACCO, ETC.,

High Street, Chestertown, Md.

Enoch Latham,
BOOT AND SHOE MAKER,

Chestertown, Md., Opposite M. E. Church.

BOOTS AND SHOES MADE TO ORDER.   SATISFACTION GUARANTEED.

All kinds of REPAIRING at Special Low Prices.

A call solicited.   ENOCH LATHAM.

POLK & BENSON,

FINE MERCHANT TAILORING AT LOW PRICES,

POCOMOKE CITY, MARYLAND.

——— IMPORTED NOVELTIES IN ———

SCOTCH AND ENGLISH

SUITINGS.

M. A. TOULSON,

Druggist.

A Well-Appointed Prescription Drug Store.

MOST APPROVED METHODS.

Proprietary Medicines.   M. A. TOULSON.

GO 2 NO. 212

——— FOR YOUR ———

Confectionery, Fruits

AND FAMILY GROCERIES.

WM. S. McDONNELL, CHESTERTOWN, MD.

THE NEW ENGLAND
BUREAU OF EDUCATION.

3 Somerset St., (Room 5) Boston, Mass.

This Bureau is the oldest in New England, and has gained a national reputation. We receive calls for teachers of every grade, and from every State and Territory and from abroad. During the administration of its present Manager, he has secured to its members, in salaries, an aggregate of $1,500,000, yet calls for teachers have never been so numerous as during the current year.

Ten teachers have been elected from this Bureau, the current year, in one New England city, viz.: Grammar (male), $2000; Grammar (male), $2000; Grammar (male), $2000; three Manuel Training (males), $3000; Sciences (male), $1600; Elocution and Physical Culture (female), $900; Kindergarten Critic (female), $750; Domestic Sciences (female), $1100. Aggregate Salaries $11,950.

DR. ORCUTT.   FAIRHAVEN, MASS., Sept. 19, 1894.

I desire to express to you the gratitude of our committee for your success in selecting and engaging the four teachers you have sent us. Your judgment is unerring; each teacher so eminently fills the requirement. We made no mistake in placing the matter—*carte blanche*—in your hands; and for the success of the past we shall be only too glad to ask your assistance in the future, assured that your selections will not disappoint us.
Cordially yours,   C. C. CUNDALL, Chairman, S. C.

MY DEAR MR. ORCUTT:—   FAIRHAVEN, MASS., Dec. 10, 1894.

You see I come again for another teacher, which proves conclusively that we are pleased and satisfied with the others you sent us. All four of them are exceptionally good, and doing work worthy of the commendation they receive from both the superintendent and committee.
I enclose signed contract for another teacher. Engage the teacher you are satisfied with for me, and fill the name blank, and I SHALL THEN KNOW just the teacher I want is coming.   Cordially yours,   C. C. CUNDALL, M. D., Chairman School Committee.

WE HAVE HAD THIRTY SUCH CALLS THIS SEASON.

☞ Teachers seeking positions or promotion should register at once. No charge to school officers for services tendered. Forms and circulars free.
Address or call upon   HIRAM ORCUTT, MANAGER.

Sanders & Stayman,

934 F. STREET, N.W., WASHINGTON. D.C.   **13 N. CHARLES ST.,** BALTIMORE. MD.

Leading Music House.

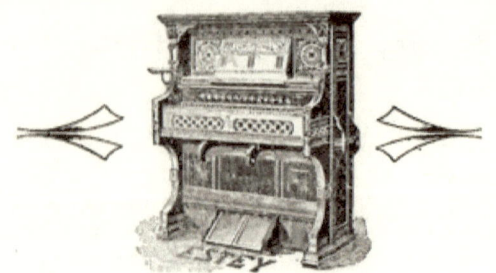

STANDARD PIANOS AND ORGANS.

THE ESTEY ORGAN.

ESTEY ORGANS.—Immeasurably superior to all others.

THE PHONORIUM is the greatest development in organ-making, and is the admiration of Organists who have examined it.

LYON & HEALY CHURCH ORGAN is a substitute for the large pipe organ, and costs less than half as much.

WEBER PIANOS.—The delight of artists.

DECKER BROTHERS' PIANOS.—Nothing finer can be found.

ESTEY PIANOS.—A great success. The name enough.

FISCHER PIANOS.—Nearly 100,000. A record unparalleled.

IVERS & POND PIANOS are truly magnificent, and are attracting the widest attention.

THE ÆOLIAN is the most wonderful musical instrument of the age. Any one with a week's practice can play any piece of music written. Concerts daily.

Leading makes of GUITARS, BANJOS, MANDOLINS, CORNETS, VIOLINS and Instruments of all kinds.

A Splendid Stock of Sheet Music Books, etc.

www.ingramcontent.com/pod-product-compliance
Lightning Source LLC
Chambersburg PA
CBHW022132160426
43197CB00009B/1248